PARC OLYMPIQUE
AND THE NORTH

Jardin
Botanique
de Montréal

Biodôme de
Montréal

Parc
Olympique

MAISONNEUVE

PRÉFONTAINE

HOCHELAGA

ST-EUSÈBE

STE-MARIE

TERRASSE
ONTARIO

PAPINEAU

La Ronde

Île
Sainte-Hélène

ST-JACQUES

La Biosphère

Lieu Historique National
George-Étienne Cartier

Chapelle
Notre-Dame-
de-Bonsecours

VIEUX-MONTRÉAL
AND THE PORT

Marché
Bonsecours

Basilique
Notre-Dame

Vieux-Port-
de Montréal

Île Notre-
Dame

St Patrick's
Basilica

VIEUX-MONTRÉAL

Pointe-à-Callière

Saint-Laurent

Centre d'Histoire
de Montréal

DOWNTOWN

POINTE-ST-CHARLES

ST-GABRIEL

CITYPACK TOP 25
Montréal

TIM JEPSON

If you have any comments
or suggestions for this guide
you can contact the editor at
Citypack@theAA.com

AA Publishing
Find out more about AA Publishing and the wide
range of services the AA provides by visiting our
website at www.theAA.com/travel

How to Use This Book

KEY TO SYMBOLS

✚ Map reference to the accompanying fold-out map

✉ Address

☎ Telephone number

🕐 Opening/closing times

🍴 Restaurant or café

🚆 Nearest rail station

Ⓜ Nearest subway (Metro) station

🚌 Nearest bus route

⛴ Nearest riverboat or ferry stop

♿ Facilities for visitors with disabilities

❓ Other practical information

▷ Further information

ℹ Tourist information

✋ Admission charges: Expensive (over $10), Moderate ($6–10), and Inexpensive ($5 or less)

⭐ Major Sight   ★ Minor Sight

👣 Walks   🚍 Excursions

🛍 Shops

🎭 Entertainment and Nightlife

🍴 Restaurants

This guide is divided into four sections

• Essential Montréal: an introduction to the city and tips on making the most of your stay.

• Montréal by Area: We've broken the city into five areas, and recommended the best sights, shops, entertainment venues, nightlife and restaurants in each one. Suggested walks help you to explore on foot.

• Where to Stay: the best hotels, whether you're looking for luxury, budget or something in between.

• Need to Know: the info you need to make your trip run smoothly, including getting about by public transport, weather tips, emergency phone numbers and useful websites.

Navigation In the Montréal by Area chapter, we've given each area its own color, which is also used on the locator maps throughout the book and the map on the inside front cover.

Maps The fold-out map accompanying this book is a comprehensive street plan of Montréal. The grid on this fold-out map is the same as the grid on the locator maps within the book. We've given grid references within the book for each sight and listing.

Contents

Introducing Montréal

Montréal is one of the world's great cities, a stylish, and laid-back metropolis, boasting superb museums, excellent restaurants, first-rate shopping, a vibrant cultural life and a cosmopolitan population that works and plays with a broad smile on its face.

Nestled between the banks of the St. Lawrence River and the slopes of Mont-Royal, the heart of the island city is a wonderful mixture of old and new: from the cobbled streets, historic squares and fine buildings of the Vieux-Port, the city's earliest incarnation after the arrival of French settlers in 1642, to the busy modern streets of Downtown, with its many gleaming skyscrapers and dazzling underground malls and walkways. Farther afield is the site of the 1976 Olympic Games, now an attraction in its own right.

Montréal, of course, owes much of its considerable charm—not least its superb food—to its French heritage, one that has made it the largest French-speaking city in the West after Paris. But to focus only on the city's French élan would be to miss the dynamic influence of its English-speaking and thriving immigrant populations, and the joie de vivre of a city that is young at heart.

True, there are problems—the winters can be cruel—but the old concerns of language, and of Montréal and the rest of Québec splitting from Canada, have receded. And Montréal is not just about food, fashion and entertainment, of style over substance. The fur trade and river traffic that made it rich may have declined, but this is still an economic powerhouse, still a place with a little grit to go with its wit.

So, a little piece of Europe in North America? Up to a point. French in taste? Definitely. English? In places, certainly. Canadian? That too. But also a dynamic, fun and fascinating city in its own right—whatever your language and whatever your fancy.

Facts + Figures

Population: 1,812,540 (in 2001)
Percentage of population that is French-speaking: 54
Ranking: Canada's second-largest city after Toronto
Area of city: 483sq km (188sq miles)
Islands making up city: 75

PRINTED PAGE

Mordecai Richler brings the vibrant, hard-scrabble life of Montréal's Jewish community to life in the classic *St. Urban's Horseman* and *The Apprenticeship of Duddy Kravitz* (made into a film starring Richard Dreyfuss). Gabrielle Roy captured the struggles of the French-speaking population in *Bonheur d'Occasion* (translated as The Tin Flute).

BALCONVILLE

Many Montréalers live in duplexes and triplexes, stacked residences built in the 1930s and 1940s to house the city's blue-collar workers. Curving, wrought-iron staircases link the balconies of the various levels, a building strategy that saved interior space and inadvertently created pleasing places to gather round in the summer.

FAMOUS MONTRÉALERS

Montréal's famous include Star Trek's William Shatner, jazz great Oscar Peterson, novelist Mordecai Richler, film director Denys Arcand and poet-singer Leonard Cohen. Confederate president Jefferson Davis lived in the city briefly after the American Civil War and singer Céline Dion was born in Repentigny.

A Short Stay in Montréal

DAY 1

Morning Begin your day in **Place Jacques-Cartier** (▷ 37) in Vieux-Montréal. Walk southwest on rue Notre-Dame Ouest and visit the **Basilique Notre-Dame** (▷ 24–25). Spend the rest of the morning learning about the history of the city in the **Centre d'Histoire de Montréal** (▷ 27) and nearby **Musée d'Archéologie et d'Histoire de Montréal** (▷ 32). If time allows before lunch, visit the quirky **Musée Marc-Aurèle Fortin** (▷ 37).

Lunch Have a snack at **Olive et Gourmando** (▷ 44), a light meal in **L'Arrivage Café** (▷ 33) in the Musée d'archéologie, or sample one of the many casual restaurants in the **Vieux-Port** area (▷ 34).

Afternoon If the weather is good, take a boat trip from one of the quays a few moments from the Musée d'archéologie. Most last an hour or 90 minutes. If you are travelling with children you may want to visit the **iSci science centre** (▷ 34) and other attractions on the waterfront piers. Then explore the Vieux-Port area northwest of Place Jacques-Cartier, especially the **Chapelle Notre-Dame-de-Bonsecours** (▷ 28), **Lieu Historique National Sir George-Étienne Cartier** (▷ 29) and **Château Ramezay** (▷ 35). The café in the latter makes a delightful place for afternoon tea. Also make time for shopping in the **Marché Bonsecours** (▷ 30) and the stores along rue Saint-Paul Est.

Dinner Try **Toqué!** (▷ 44), one of Montréal's best restaurants for contemporary cuisine, but be sure to book well in advance. If you want to eat outdoors, reserve a terrace table at **Boris Bistro** (▷ 43).

Evening Take in a performance at the **Centaur Theatre** (▷ 42) or enjoy a drink with a waterfront view at **Pub St-Paul** (▷ 42). If the circus is in town, try for last-minute tickets at **Cirque du Soleil** (▷ 42).

DAY 2

Morning Take a cab close to the Observatoire de l'Est in the **Parc du Mont-Royal** (▷ 72–73) for an overview of the city and a taste of Montréal's main park. Walk through the park to Avenue des Pins and then visit the **McCord Museum** (▷ 52–53) and **Musée des Beaux-Arts** (▷ 74). Fill any time before lunch by exploring shops and malls such as La Baie and Centre Eaton above and below ground near rue Sainte-Catherine.

Lunch Downtown has many sandwich bars and inexpensive restaurants aimed at the area's working population. For a slice of historic Montréal, eat at **Bens** (▷ 65). Otherwise try **Ambiance** (▷ 65) for interesting pasta dishes, or if you prefer something lighter such as a salad.

Afternoon If you are getting tired, devote the afternoon to the sights and shops of Downtown. If not, take the green Métro line to Pie-IX or Viau to see the sights on and around the **Parc Olympique** (▷ 87), especially the **Biodôme** (▷ 88) and **Jardin Botanique** (▷ 90).

Dinner You have two choices for dinner if you don't want to return to Vieux-Montréal. Busier and younger is the Quartier Latin, one of the city's main areas for eating, drinking and nightlife. More sedate is boulevard Saint-Laurent above rue Sherbrooke, where you could try **Moishe's** (▷ 82), which has been serving sublime steaks since 1938, or the fashionable **Globe** (▷ 81–82), for more contemporary food.

Evening Walk from rue Sherbrooke to the Quartier Latin to enjoy its boisterous nightlife or, when in season, attend a ballet or a concert by Montréal's Orchestre Métropolitain. Additionally, during the summer, there will always be a festival of some sort taking place somewhere in the city.

Top 25

These pages are a quick guide to the Top 25, which are described in more detail later. Here they are listed alphabetically and the tinted background shows the area they are in.

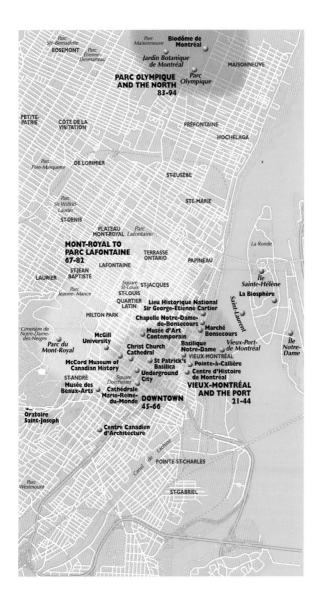

Parc Ste-Bernadette
ROSEMONT
Parc Étienne-Desmarteau
Parc Maisonneuve
Biodôme de Montréal
Jardin Botanique de Montréal
MAISONNEUVE
PARC OLYMPIQUE AND THE NORTH 83-94
Parc Olympique

PETITE-PATRIE
CÔTE DE LA VISITATION
PRÉFONTAINE
HOCHELAGA

Parc Père-Marquette
DE LORIMIER
ST-EUSÈBE

Parc Sir Wilfrid-Laurier
STE-MARIE

ST-DENIS
PLATEAU MONT-ROYAL
Parc Lafontaine

MONT-ROYAL TO PARC LAFONTAINE 67-82
TERRASSE ONTARIO
LAFONTAINE
La Ronde

ST-JEAN BAPTISTE
Parc Jeanne-Mance
Square St-Louis
ST-JACQUES
PAPINEAU
Île Sainte-Hélène
La Biosphère

LAURIER
ST-LOUIS
QUARTIER LATIN
MILTON PARK
Lieu Historique National Sir George-Étienne Cartier
Chapelle Notre-Dame-de-Bonsecours
Marché Bonsecours
Musée d'Art Contemporain
VIEUX-MONTRÉAL
Vieux-Port-de Montréal
Île Notre-Dame

Cimetière de Notre-Dame-des-Neiges
McGill University
Christ Church Cathedral
Basilique Notre-Dame
Parc du Mont-Royal
McCord Museum of Canadian History
St Patrick's Basilica
Pointe-à-Callière
Centre d'Histoire de Montréal

ST-ANDRÉ
Square Dorchester
Underground City
VIEUX-MONTRÉAL AND THE PORT 21-44

Musée des Beaux-Arts
Cathédrale Marie-Reine-du-Monde
DOWNTOWN 45-66

Oratoire Saint-Joseph

Centre Canadien d'Architecture

Parc Westmount
Canal de Lachine
POINTE-ST-CHARLES

ST-GABRIEL

Shopping

Le shopping—now there's a word that crosses linguistic boundaries. Some Québécois may still *magasinent*, but the truly stylish *font le shopping*.

A Passion for Fashion

And Montréal is nothing if not stylish. The women dress well and, more tellingly, so do the men. Montréal is Canada's fashion capital, with a clothing industry that employs 70,000 people. Several fashion schools churn out talent to challenge the leadership of Léo Chevalier, Michel Robichaud and John Warden. And if you're looking for children's clothes, this is the place. Shoppers can find all the best stuff in the city's boutiques and department stores, but the bargain hunter seeks out the little factories that sell goods to the public on Saturday mornings.

Outdoor Clothing

In the same vein—but less politically correct—is the fur industry. Trade in animal skins made the city wealthy in the first place, and given the climate, it's not surprising that furs are still popular winter wear. However, some designers have taken a less traditional approach to cold-weather wear. The multilayer winter wear of Kanuk (▷ 79) is stylish and comfortable.

Antiques

Montréal's age makes it a tempting prospect for antiques collectors. Dozens of shops in Westmount, along the west end of rue Notre-

---

TASTEFUL SOUVENIRS

Try such local delicacies as smoked meat and bagels. Markets stock a variety of Québec cheeses—chèvres, bries and sharp cheddars. Some of the finest are made by the Benedictine monks of Saint Benoît de Lac. Trappist monks in the Lac Saint-Jean region make another favorite: chocolate-covered blueberries. For meatier items look for jars of Canards Lac-Brome pâtés and confit, as well as packages of smoked duck breast. For a sweet gift pick up some maple syrup.

From antiques shops and stylish shopping areas to bustling street markets, you can shop till you drop

Le Centre Eaton (top). Mouth-watering pastries (middle). Maple syrup, an ideal souvenir (bottom)

Dame and in the Village cater to just about every taste, with furniture from colonial Québec to 1950s retro. Keep an eye out for rare books in both languages, as well as Victorian paintings, religious articles and decorations, china and silverware. Many shops also stock English and European antiques.

Arts and Crafts

Québec's artistic traditions reach back to the days of New France, when the colony's Catholic bishops kept dozens of artists hard at work, decorating churches with mosaics, paintings, sculptures and stained glass. Dozens of galleries service more modern tastes, with work by leading local artists like Paul Fenniak, Betty Goodwin and Jean-Louis Émond. If your tastes lean more to the traditional, consider a startlingly realistic wood carving by a Québec folk artist or a graceful soapstone sculpture by one of Canada's Inuit carvers.

Malls and Department Stores

While trendy shopping areas such as rue-Saint Denis, rue Sherbrooke in Downtown and boulevard Saint-Laurent take the retail plaudits, don't overlook the joys of one-stop shopping under a single roof. Montréal makes a great place for pre-Christmas shopping, thanks to the many malls and stores in its Underground City, which provides essential protection from the elements. The rest of the year, the malls—most of which are in Downtown—are equally appealing, as are classic department stores.

A GOOD SMOKE

Canada has never severed diplomatic or trade relations with Cuba, and so just about every tobacconist in Montréal has a humidor full of Havanas—something you won't find anywhere south of the US border. But be careful: US laws embargo trade with Cuba and trying to take goods across the border could lead to charges. Visitors from elsewhere, however, can take a handsome Montecristo home if they so wish.

Shopping by Theme

Whether you're looking for a department store, a quirky boutique, or something in between, you'll find it all in Montréal. On this page shops are listed by theme. For a more detailed write-up, see the individual listings in Montréal by Area.

ACCESSORIES

Birks (▷ 62)
Brown Chaussures (▷ 62)
Henri Henri (▷ 62–63)

ART AND ANTIQUES

Galerie des Arts Relais des
   Époques (▷ 40)
Galerie le Chariot (▷ 40)
Guilde Canadienne des
   Métiers d'Art (▷ 78–79)
La Guilde Graphique
   (▷ 41)
Petit Musée (▷ 63)

BOOKS AND MUSIC

Archambault (▷ 78)
HMV (▷ 79)
Indigo (▷ 63)
Paragraphe Book Store
   (▷ 63)
Steve's Music Store
   (▷ 41)
Ulysses La Librairie du
   Voyage (▷ 63)
Université McGill (▷ 79)
The Word (▷ 63)

CLOTHES

Aime Com Moi (▷ 78)
Chapafolie (▷ 78)
Chas Johnson & Sons
   (▷ 62)
Dubuc Mode de Vie
   (▷ 78)
Giorgio (▷ 78)
Griff 3000 (▷ 40)
Nadya Toto (▷ 79)
Ogilvy (▷ 79)
Roots (▷ 63)
Scarlett O'Hara (▷ 79)

CRAFT AND DESIGN

Botique des Métiers d'Art
   du Québec (▷ 40)
Desmarais et Robitaille
   (▷ 40)
L'Empreinte Coopérative
   (▷ 40)
L'Institut de Design (▷ 41)

GIFTS AND TOYS

Bella Pella (▷ 78)
Canadian Maple Delights
   (▷ 40)
Edifice Belgo (▷ 62)
Kanuk (▷ 79)
Pointe-à-Callière (▷ 41)
Vale d'Coeur (▷ 79)
Worn Doorstep (▷ 41)

MALLS/DEPT. STORES

La Baie (▷ 62)
Le Centre Eaton (▷ 62)
Complexe Desjardins
   (▷ 62)
Les Cours Mont-Royal
   (▷ 78)
Le Faubourg Sainte-
   Catherine (▷ 78)
Holt Renfrew (▷ 79)
Marché Bonsecours
   (▷ 41)
Place Ville-Marie (▷ 63)
Promenades de la
   Cathédrale (▷ 63)
Simons (▷ 63)

Montréal by Night

Montréalers never hibernate, no matter how cold it gets. Saturday-night crowds are almost as large in January as they are in July.

Hot Spots

Crowds congregate in two main districts, each with its own ambience. In one of these areas—downtown—the scene is mainly on four streets that run between boulevard René-Lévesque and rue Sherbrooke—de la Montagne, Crescent, Bishop and Mackay. They're lined with fine old graystone residences now converted into pubs, clubs and bistros, which appeal to a young, hip and largely English-speaking crowd. Just as vibrant but more French in ambience is the district around the twin corridors of boulevard Saint-Laurent and rue Saint-Denis. Start around rue Sainte-Catherine and walk away from the river through the Quartier Latin and Plateau Mont-Royal, exploring the cafés and clubs on Prince-Arthur and Rachel. There's plenty of entertainment here for all ages and you'll find both languages everywhere.

Evening Stroll

Vieux-Montréal has only a few nightclubs, but it's a wonderful place for an evening stroll. Many of the old classical buildings, including the Hôtel de Ville, Place Royale and the Château Ramezay, are beautifully illuminated, and a small section of rue Sainte-Hélène is lighted by gas lamps.

LONG HISTORY

Montréal has been a popular hot spot with Americans since at least the 1920s and 1930s. During Prohibition, trainloads of fun-seekers from New York and Boston would pour into the city every weekend looking for some excitement and a little legal booze. The city was also popular with African-American jazz musicians, who liked the fact they could pretty much stay and eat wherever they wanted—and date locals without raising much more than an eyebrow.

Party all night at a club, try your luck in a casino, pay a visit to the ballet, or take in some jazz

Eating Out

Montréal is one of North America's gastronomic capitals, a city that is passionate
about its food, and which draws on French
and other ethnic culinary influences to offer
a wonderfully rich assortment of restaurants, cafés and cuisines.

French Tastes
France is the obvious point of culinary reference,
and French-influenced food is the city's most
widespread, found not only in restaurants that
wouldn't be out of place in Paris, but also in a
plethora of cafés and bistros in settings every bit
as Gallic as their European counterparts.

Plenty of Choice
The city's rich and multicultural population provides the inspiration for countless other
cuisines—from Thai, Vietnamese and Korean to
Indian, Chinese and Italian. Not forgetting the
classic staples of North America, with some
excellent steak houses, plenty of places for
pasta, chicken and seafood, and one or two
timeless diners and delis for bagels and the like.

Where to Go
The key dining areas are well defined, the most
popular being rue Saint-Denis and boulevard
Saint-Laurent between rue Sherbrooke and rue
Mont-Royal. Here, as in Vieux-Montréal, you are
spoiled for choice, though the downtown area,
too, has plenty to offer. Also, explore the Village,
along rue Notre-Dame.

PRACTICALITIES

At lunch, look out for set-price two-or three-course menus
known as the *spécial du midi*, or midday special. These are
good value, as are the two- to four-course set *table d'hôte*
menus in the evening. These menus will usually be better
value than eating à la carte. A multi-course *menu dégusta-
cion*, or tasting menu, will be expensive, but will offer a
selection of dishes in small portions, often accompanied by
different wines. A starter, or appetizer, in Montréal is called
an *entrée*, and the main course is the *plat principal*.

*In a city very much influ-
enced by the French, expect
to find many atmospheric
street cafés and bistros*

Restaurants by Cuisine

There are restaurants to suit all tastes and budgets in Montréal. On this page they are listed by cuisine. For a more detailed description of each restaurant, see Montréal by Area.

CAFÉS/PÂTISSERIES

Ambiance (▷ 65)
La Brioche Lyonnaise
 (▷ 81)
Café du Château (▷ 43)
Café Santropol (▷ 81)
Claude Postel (▷ 44)
Les Gâtieres Café (▷ 81)
Olive et Gourmando
 (▷ 44)
Pâtisseries Belge (▷ 82)
Saint-Viateur Bagel & Café
 (▷ 82)

CONTEMPORARY

Aix Cuisine du Terroir
 (▷ 43)
Chez L'Épicier (▷ 44)
Cube (▷ 44)
Globe (▷ 81–82)
Toque! (▷ 44)

ETHNIC CUISINE

L'Actuel (▷ 65)
Café Ferrari (▷ 81)
Café Stash(▷ 43)
Phaya Thai (▷ 82)
La Taj (▷ 66)

FRENCH

À La Découverte (▷ 81)
Auberge le Saint-Gabriel
 (▷ 43)
Au Bistro Gourmet
 (▷ 65)
Bonaparte (▷ 43)
Boris Bistro (▷ 43)
Les Caprices de Nicholas
 (▷ 65)
Le Caveau (▷ 65)
Chez La Mère Michel
 (▷ 65)
L'Express (▷ 81)
La Loux (▷ 82)
Le Mas des Oliviers
 (▷ 66)
Le Paris (▷ 66)
La Rapiere (▷ 66)
Restaurant Julien (▷ 66)

ITALIAN AND GREEK

Cavalli (▷ 65)
Da Emma (▷ 44)
Le Jardin de Panos
 (▷ 82)
Le Latini (▷ 65)
Psarotaverna du
Symposium (▷ 82)

PAN-ASIAN CUISINE

Bon Blé Riz (▷ 81)
Chu Chai (▷ 81)
Nagoya (▷ 44)
Orchidée de Chine
 (▷ 66)
Ruby Rouge (▷ 66)

QUICK AND LIGHT

À L'Aventure (▷ 43)
Bens (▷ 65)
Eggspectation (▷ 44)

STEAK AND FISH

Au Pied de Cochon
 (▷ 81)
Le Bourlingueur (▷ 43)
Entrecôte Saint-Jean
 (▷ 65)
Moishe's (▷ 82)
Mr. Steer (▷ 66)
La Paryse (▷ 82)
Queue de Cheval (▷ 66)
Schwaratz's (▷ 82)

If You Like...

However you'd like to spend your time in Montréal, these top suggestions should help you tailor your ideal visit. Each sight or listing has a fuller write-up in Montréal by Area.

BURNING THE MIDNIGHT OIL

Board a nighttime cruise with disco on the St. Lawrence river (▷ 26).
Visit the clubs of the Village and Quartier Latin (▷ 80).
Join the revelers in one of Downtown's Irish bars (▷ 64).

THE LAP OF LUXURY

Stay on the "Gold Floor" of the Fairmont La Reine Elizabeth hotel (▷ 110).
Eat at Toque!, one of the city's finest restaurants (▷ 44).
Go mad among the designer labels showcased within the Holt Renfrew (▷ 79) department store or in the designer shops on avenue Laurier at the north end of Parc du Mont-Royal.

Downtown gets lively after dark (above). Powerboat rafting (middle). Jazz features at many of the summer festivals (bottom)

TO KEEP YOUR CHILDREN HAPPY

Take them to a performance of Cirque du Soleil (▷ 42).
Strap them in for a jet-boat trip over the Ladine Rapids (▷ 26).
Visit the Insectarium and Biodôme (▷ 88–89) at the Parc Olympique (▷ 87).

SAVING FOR A RAINY DAY

Visit the visitor center for details of free concerts in churches, parks, malls and the Vieux-Port (▷ 34).
Remember that some museums have free entry on certain nights.
Juste Pour Rire, the Jazz and other summer festivals have many free events (▷ 114).

Nightlife at the Sky Pub (top). Eating in style at the Casino de Montréal (bottom)

AN EVENING OF ENTERTAINMENT

Attend an ice-hockey game involving Montréal's Les Canadiens (▷ 56).

The Places des Arts plays host to several orchestras and leading ballet and opera companies (▷ 64).

Listen to jazz at Quai des Brumes (▷ 80), where there are two very different jazz clubs in one building.

A MEMORABLE PLACE TO STAY

For modern chic and contemporary styling, the Hôtel Godin and "W" hotel win hands down (▷ 112).

The Hôtel Nelligan is divinely romantic (▷ 111).

Inexpensive, central and intimate, the Auberge de la Place Royale is a quirky gem (▷ 110).

ROMANTIC SUPPERS

A typically stylish room at one of Montréal's many chic hotels

The Quartier Latin has numerous romantic little bistros (▷ 81–82).

In summer, Boris Bistro's lovely terrace is the place to eat (▷ 43).

Dining rooms at Les Caprices de Nicolas are some of the city's most sumptuous (▷ 65).

A TASTE OF TRADITION

Steaks at Moishe's have been aged and prepared the same way since 1938 (▷ 82).

Classic smoked and cured meats are the specialty of old-world Schwaratz's (▷ 82).

Grab lunch or a late-night snack at Bens, a throwback to the 1950s (▷ 65).

This is just one of Montréal's intimate French bistros

A BREATH OF FRESH AIR

Clamber to the heights of the Parc du Mont-Royal (▷ 72).
Take a turn around the Jardin Botanique (▷ 90), adjoining Parc Maisonneuve (▷ 94).
Enjoy a brisk stroll along the Vieux-Port waterfront (▷ 34).

Savor the Montréal skyline from high spots around the city

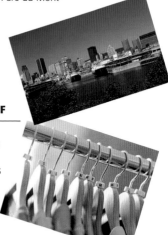

SHOPPING UNDER ONE ROOF

La Baie (▷ 62) and Simons (▷ 63) are landmark Downtown department stores.
Le Centre Eaton is Downtown's largest mall (▷ 62).
Explore the Underground City, a labyrinth of shops sheltered from the elements (▷ 56–57).

SPECIALTY SHOPPING

Marché Bonsecours (▷ 41) and nearby rue Saint-Paul (▷ 41) are excellent for traditional art, craft and design.
Explore rue Saint-Denis for cutting-edge clothes and funky stores (▷ 76).
Rue Amhurst near rue Ontario and rue Notre-Dame Ouest near rue Guy are great for antiques (▷ 40–41).

CUTTING-EDGE CULTURE

Fine arts and a fine setting define the Musée des Beaux-Arts (▷ 74).
Be shocked or amused but never bored at the Musée d'Art Contemporain (▷ 51).
Pointe-à-Callière offers Montréal's best modern museum (▷ 32).

A maze of shops all linked together by Montréal's Underground City (above)

The abstract façade of the Musée des Beaux-Arts, the oldest museum in the country

Once the heart of the ancient city, Vieux-Montréal has been transformed into a busy and revitalized area.

Square
Viger

Édifice
J-Viger

**Lieu Historique National
Sir George-Étienne Cartier**

Maison
Brossard-Gauvin

**Maison Pierre-
du-Calvet**

Bassin de
l'Horloge

**Rue
Bonsecours**

**Chapelle Notre-
Dame-de-
Bonsecours**

**Maison
Papineau**

**Château
Ramezay**

Hôtel de
Ville

**Marché
Bonsecours**

**Labyrinthe du
Hangar 16**

Pavillon et Scène
du Bassin Bonsecours

**Place
Jacques-Cartier**

Bassin Bonsecours

**Vieux
Palais de
Justice**

Rue St-Amable

Quai
Jacques-Cartier

Édifice
Ernest-
Cormier

Palais de
Justice

Bassin
Jacques-Cartier

**VIEUX-
MONTRÉAL**

Économusée

Rue St-Dizier

Images du
Future

Quai King-Edward

Centre iSci

Bassin
King-Edward

Centaur
Theatre

**Basilique
Notre-Dame**

Place Royale

Théâtre
Biscuit

Pointe-à-Callière

Quai Alexandra

Rue St-Paul

**Centre
d'Histoire
de Montréal**

Bassin
Alexandra

**Place
d'Youville**

Musée Marc-Aurèle Fortin

RUE MCGILL

Rue des Soeurs-Grises

Parc du
Moulin à
Vent

Bassin de la Pointe
du Moulin à Vent

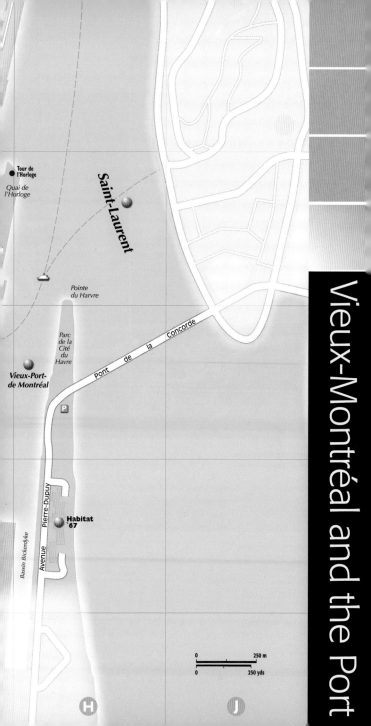

Tour de
l'Horloge

Quai de
l'Horloge

Saint-Laurent

Pointe
du Harvre

Parc
de la
Cité
du
Havre

Pont de la Concorde

Vieux-Port-
de Montréal

P

Avenue Pierre-Dupuy

Bassin Bickerdyke

Habitat
'67

0   250 m

0   250 yds

Vieux-Montréal and the Port

H   J

Basilique Notre-Dame

HIGHLIGHTS

- Pulpit
- Wood carving
- Stained glass
- High altar

TIPS

- No more than an hour is needed for a visit.
- Son et Lumière shows take place daily Tue–Thu (usually at 6.30pm) and twice daily on Fri (6.30 and 8.30pm) and Sat (7 and 8.30pm). Cost is $10 and tickets are from the "Parvis" shop in the church.

No other site in Montréal sums up the city's religious heritage as beautifully as the Basilica of Notre-Dame, where the seductive interior—Romanesque with touches of rococo—lifts you into a world of almost perfect calm.

History Founded in 1627, Notre-Dame is on the flanks of Place d'Armes, the historic focus of the old city. The original church was replaced by the present neo-Gothic basilica between 1824 and 1829. Today there is a skyscraper on the square's western side, but the church's twin towers—nicknamed Temperance and Perseverance—still command the skyline. The western tower, built in 1843, contains the famous "Gros Bourdon" bell; the bell's peal can be heard up to 25km (15 miles) away.

A lighted backdrop highlights the ornate altar of the Basilique Notre-Dame (right)
A horse-drawn carriage (caleche) pulls up outside the Basilica of Notre-Dame (left)

Highly decorated Inside, thousands of tiny 24-carat gold stars stud the dusky blue, vaulted ceiling, and 14 stained-glass windows, brought from Limoges in 1929, tell the story of Ville-Marie's early development. But most of the interior is a tribute to the woodworking skills of Québec artists and artisans. All the figures in the life-size tableaus behind the main altar are carved in wood as is the spectacular pulpit with its curving staircase on the east side of the nave. A fire in 1978 destroyed much of the large chapel behind the main altar. The Sulpician priests who run the church saved what they could of the woodwork and erected an enormous, modern bronze sculpture behind the altar. The chapel is still the most popular for weddings in Montréal; in 1994 singer Céline Dion married her manager here in a ceremony that rivaled the pomp of a royal wedding.

THE BASICS

www.basiliquenddm.org
⊞ F11
✉ 110 rue Notre-Dame Ouest
☎ Basilica 514/842–2925
🕐 Mon–Fri 8–4.30, Sat 8–4.15, Sun 12.30–4.15
Ⓟ Place-d'Armes
🚌 38, 55, 129
♿ Very good
💲 Inexpensive
❓ 20-min guided tours ($4) in French or English daily, roughly every 30 min. Organ demonstrations (Wed–Fri, $6)

Boat Trip on the St. Lawrence

Tour boats tied up to the jetty waiting for passengers to board for a short cruise

THE BASICS

🔆 G10

🚇 Champs-de-Mars, Place-d'Armes

🚌 38, 55, 61, 129

Le Bateau-Mouche
www.bateau-mouche.ca
✉ Quai Jacques-Cartier
☎ 514/849–9952

Saute Moutons
www.jetboatingmontreal.com
✉ Quai de Horloge
☎ 514/284–9607

Croisières AML
www.croisieresaml.com
✉ Quai King Edward
☎ 800/563–4643

TIPS

● Tours are popular, so be sure to book ahead.

● Safety equipment is provided on jet-boat and rafting tours, but take extra warm and waterproof clothing. Jet-boat and speed-boat tours are not recommended for pregnant women or those with back problems.

The St. Lawrence (St.-Laurent) has been Montréal's lifeblood for centuries, a vital artery for trade and communication. You can enjoy a taste of the great river on one of the short cruises or thrilling jet-boats that leave from the Vieux-Port.

The sights Three main companies operate river trips from the Vieux-Port, each providing a variety of day, evening and dining cruises. Most offer passengers views of the port area and the islands of Notre-Dame and Sainte-Hélène: a few venture further, taking in the Commune, Sainte-Marguerite and other islands beyond Longueuil. All operate daily from mid-May to October.

Plenty to choose from The best known is Le Bateau-Mouche, which operate from the Jacques-Cartier Pier, offering four sedate one-hour cruises at 10am, 1.30pm, 3pm and 4.30pm, plus a 90-minute midday cruise departing at 11.30am. Boats have a glass-enclosed passenger deck. Saute Moutons offers more exhilarating one-hour jet-boat rides over the Lachine Rapids every two hours 10am–6pm. Boats leave from the Clock Tower Pier. It also has rafting and speed-boat tours over the same stretch of wild water. Croisières AML provide a ferry transit service to Longueuil from the Old Port, plus a range of once- or twice-daily cruises aboard the 1000-person Cavalier Maxim, a former ferry. Basic day cruises last 90 minutes and leave from the King-Edward Pier. Also available are 90-minute Sunday brunch and sunset cruises and four-hour dinner cruises.

The Centre d'Histoire de Montréal, housed in the old red-brick fire station

Centre d'Histoire de Montréal

Although this history museum seems a little dated at first glance, it tells Montréal's story in an interesting way, allowing you to step in and share snippets of Montréalers' day-to-day lives from 1642 to the present.

History Of the monuments and historic sites that line Place d'Youville, one of Montréal's earliest market squares, the most attractive is the beautifully restored red-stone Caserne Centrale de Pompiers, or old Central Fire Station (1903). Today this building houses the Centre d'Histoire de Montréal, an 11-room interpretative center, which uses dioramas, videos and other media to trace the city's development from Iroquois settlement to metropolis. Look for the mock-ups of the streetcar, the 19th-century factory and the gaudy 1940s living room. Temporary exhibitions on off-beat aspects of the city's history are held upstairs.

Also on the square On the square's south side are the Youville Stables (Écuries d'Youville), graystone buildings constructed in 1828 as warehouses for grain merchants and soap manufacturers (the stables were next door). In 1967 the complex was converted into offices, shops and artisans' studios. Just off the square a plaque commemorates the Hôpital Général des Sœurs-Grises (Gray Nuns' General Hospital), founded in 1694 and taken over in 1747 by Marguerite d'Youville, the widow who founded the Sœurs Grises. The order treated the sick, poor and elderly and established one of the first foundling hospitals.

THE BASICS

www.ville.montreal.qc.ca/chm

F12

335 place d'Youville

514/872–3207

Tue–Sun 10–5

Square-Victoria, Place-d'Armes

38, 55, 61

Moderate

Guided tours need to be arranged in advance

HIGHLIGHTS

- Fire Station building
- Tram car
- Youville Stables

Chapelle Notre-Dame-de-Bonsecours

Glorious statues adorn the Chapelle Notre-Dame-de-Bonsecours, inside and out

THE BASICS

www.marguerite-bourgeoys.com
⊞ G10
✉ 400 rue Saint-Paul Est
☎ 514/282–8670
🕐 May–Oct Tue–Sun 10–5.30; Nov–mid-Jan and Mar–Apr Tue–Sun 11–3.30
Ⓜ Champ-de-Mars
🚌 38
♿ Poor: four steps to church; no access to tower or museum
💲 Chapel free. Museum moderate
❓ Small gift shop

HIGHLIGHTS

- Gold Madonna
- Murals
- Votive boats
- Mosaic inlays
- Madonna de Bonsecours
- "Aerial"
- Views

This tiny building is a monument to Marguerite Bourgeoys, a pious woman dedicated to bringing Christian civilization to New France. She founded a religious order, set up schools and built this church.

Chapel St. Marguerite Bourgeoys picked the site for the chapel in 1657, just outside Ville-Marie's stockade, and persuaded Montréal's founder, Paul de Chomedey, Sieur de Maisonneuve, to help with the project. The original building was destroyed by fire, and the present stone edifice dates from 1771. The 1998 renovation revealed some beautiful 18th-century murals.

A sailors haunt The chapel has always had a special place in the hearts of mariners. Situated on the waterfront, it was built to house a small 17th-century statue of Notre-Dame-de-Bonsecours (Our Lady of Good Hope), credited with the rescue of those in peril at sea. A larger-than-life statue of the Virgin graces the steeple of the present building, facing the river with arms outstretched in welcome. Mariners who survived ocean crossings in the 18th and 19th centuries often came to the church to thank the Virgin for her help, and to leave votive lamps in the shape of small model ships. Many of them still hang from the ceiling and the chapel is usually referred to simply as the Église des Matelots, the Sailors' Church. Visitors can climb the steeple to the "Aerial," a tiny chapel where mariners came to pray. In the museum you can learn about St. Marguerite Bourgeoys.

Life as it was inside Cartier's home (left). A portrait of Sir George-Étienne Cartier (right)

Lieu Historique National Sir G.-É. Cartier

With great charm, numerous original furnishings and objects beautifully re-create the ambience of domestic life in mid 19th-century Montréal in the former home of Sir George-Étienne Cartier (1814–1873).

The man himself Sir George-Étienne Cartier, one of the founding fathers of Canadian confederation, played a large part in persuading French Canada to join the fledgling nation in 1867. In his youth Cartier had thrown his support behind the abortive 1837 rebellion against British rule, but later he became convinced that the new Canadian federation would give French Canadians the means they needed to safeguard their religion, language and culture.

Two sections The museum consists of two connected houses, which were home to the Cartier family between 1848 and 1872. The western half covers Cartier's political and industrial preoccupations. He successfully promoted the construction of the Grand Trunk Railway; He worked on the abolition of Québec's seigneurial system (a hangover from the French regime) and the rewriting of its civil code; and he was Canada's first minister of defense. In one exhibit, you can sit in at a negotiating session with Cartier and the other Fathers of Confederation. The house on the east side of the museum uses ornate period furnishings to re-create the life of the Cartier family in 19th-century Montréal. You can listen in on the servants gossiping about their masters.

THE BASICS

www.pc.gc.ca/cartier

🔹 G10

✉ 458 rue Notre-Dame Est, corner of rue Berri

☎ 514/283–2282 or 800/463–6769

🕐 Late May–Aug daily 10–6; Sep–late May Wed–Sun 10–12, 1–5

🚇 Champ-de-Mars

🚌 38

♿ Very good, but visitors using wheelchairs should call one day in advance

💰 Moderate

❓ Guided tours

HIGHLIGHTS

● Commentaries
● Sound effects
● Life-size models
● Canopied bed

TOP 25

29

Marché Bonsecours

HIGHLIGHTS

● Silver dome
● Facade
● Portico

TIPS

● For coffee, sandwiches, snacks and light meals visit Le Petit Payson inside the market.

● The Institut de Design Montréal Gallery (▷ 41) is one of the 15 stores and galleries specializing in high-quality art and design items.

The silvery dome of the Marché Bonsecours has been a landmark on the Montréal waterfront for well over a century. It serves as a reminder of the city's importance as a busy port during the 19th century.

In the beginning The site of the Marché Bonsecours was important in 18th-century New France. Colonial authorities had an administrative center here and the Marché Neuf, built to replace Montréal's first market in Place Royale, was nearby. The present building was never meant to serve as a market. The British erected it between 1845 and 1850 to fill cultural and political needs: The city councillors met downstairs and musicians played in the concert hall upstairs. It was only in 1878, when the mayor and city legislators moved to

Marché Bonsecours beautifully illuminated at night (left) and seen from a different perspective with snow on the ground (right)

their new home on rue Notre-Dame, that it became a market and remained so until the early 1960s. After a 1963 redevelopment, the building served again as municipal offices until May 1996, when it reopened as a shopping arcade.

Today The present graystone building is one of the most graceful in the city. Its long neoclassical facade, punctuated by rows of white-painted sash windows, stretches for two blocks. The main portico, supported by six cast-iron Doric columns, fronts on cobbled rue Saint-Paul in the heart of the old city. Artists and artisans display their wares in shops and stalls on the lower level and the upper floor is used for exhibits on Montréal's marine history, and for concerts and banquets. The back door opens on the Vieux-Port (▷ 34). In summer there is an outdoor café at street level.

THE BASICS

www.marchebonsecours.qc.ca

🞤 G10

✉ 350 rue Saint-Paul Est at rue Bonsecours

☎ 514/872-7730

🕐 Jan–Mar daily 10–6; Apr–late Jun and Nov–Dec Sat–Wed 10–6, Thu 10–9; late Jun–Labor Day daily 10–9; Labor Day–Oct Sun–Wed 10–6, Thu–Sat 10–9

🚇 Champ-de-Mars 🚍 38

♿ Very good 🎟 Free

Pointe-à-Callière

HIGHLIGHTS

- Virtual Exhibition
- Montréal Love Stories
- Gardening, Montréal Style
- Youville Dumping Station
- Where Montréal Was Born
- Multimedia Show

TIPS

- Allow 1–2 hours for a visit.
- Admission includes free 90-minute guided tours (weekends only).
- Check website for temporary exhibitions.

Of all the innovations in the Vieux-Port, the superb Musée d'Archéologie et d'Histoire de Montréal at Pointe-à-Callière is the most impressive. It is the best of the developments that have given a little heart to old Montréal.

Archaeology and history Visit this magnificent museum on your first morning in Montréal: It provides a fascinating introduction to the city's history, and it is also built at Pointe-à-Callière where Montréal's first 53 settlers landed from France on May 17, 1642. The museum uses audiovisual displays to tell the story of Montréal's development as a trading and meeting place.

Underground The main building of this $27-million museum is the stark, shiplike Édifice de

One of the most impressive attractions in the Vieux-Port area, the Musée d'Archéologie et d'Histoire de Montréal has put Pointe-à-Callière well and truly on the map

l'Eperon, built on the foundations of the Royal Insurance building. It houses offices, temporary exhibits, a café with river views, and a theater with a 16-minute multimedia show on Montréal's history. But its real treasures are underground. The museum gives access to the excavations underneath, where archaeologists have burrowed into the silt and rock to expose the layers of the past. They've uncovered the remains of a 19th-century sewer system, 18th-century tavern foundations and a cemetery dating to 1643. As you explore, you have virtual encounters with some of the city's more colorful citizens. Tunnels connect the excavations to the neoclassical Old Customs House, where there are more exhibits and a gift shop. The museum also incorporates the Company 4 Pumphouse, the city's first electrical water-pumping system.

THE BASICS

www.pacmusee.qc.ca

➕ F11

✉ 350 place Royale

☎ 514/872–9150

🕐 Late Jun–early Sep Tue–Fri 10–6, Sat, Sun 11–6. Early Sep–late Jun Tue–Fri 10–5, Sat, Sun 11–5

🍴 L'Arrivage Café

🚇 Place-d'Armes

🚌 38, 55, 61

♿ Very good (uneven floor downstairs)

💷 Expensive

❓ Guided tours, gift shop

Vieux-Port de Montréal

TOP 25

The Vieux-Port waterfront (left). A decorative clock tower at the Old Port (right)

THE BASICS

www.oldportofmontreal.com

www.isci.ca

➕ H11

✉ Access across old rail tracks at points along rue de la Commune

☎ 514/496–PORT or 800/971–PORT. Centre iSci 514/496–4724

🕐 Varies with attraction. Centre iSci Mon–Fri 8.30–5, Sat–Sun 9–5, plus 10–9 Fri and Sat mid-Jun to end Aug

🍽 Place Jacques-Cartier, Maison des Éclusiers and Pointe-à-Callière

🚇 Champ-de-Mars, Place-d'Armes, Square-Victoria

🚌 38, 55, 61, 129

♿ Good

💲 Free access to site. Centre iSci expensive

HIGHLIGHTS

● iSci
● IMAX-TELLS Theatre
● Jet boating
● La Tour de l'Horloge
● Harbor cruises
● People-watching

Montréal's old port has been transformed from a tangle of rusting rail lines and crumbling warehouses into one of the city's most popular parks, with bicycle trails, lawns, cafés and a state-of-the-art science center.

Seaways Although Montréal is nearly 1,600km (1,000 miles) from the sea, its position at the confluence of the Ottawa and St. Lawrence rivers made it an important trading port—a gateway to the Great Lakes cities of Canada and the US and the fur- and mineral-rich territory of the northwest. The old harbor bustled until the 1970s, when huge container ships rendered it obsolete. Shipping operations moved downriver and the port sank into decay.

Instant hit Vieux-Port is popular: In winter the February Fête des Neiges attracts thousands, and the huge skating rink is always in use. In summer the promenade is alive with strollers, skateboarders, cyclists and street performers. You can rent bicycles, in-line skates and paddle boats. Private operators offer harbor cruises and jet-boat rides on the Lachine Rapids (▷ 26). A ferry takes foot passengers to the park on Île Sainte-Hélène (▷ 101). The King Edward Pier is the home of the Centre iSci; the innovative center combines education (interactive science displays, technology exhibits and three IMAX theaters), restaurants and shopping. At the eastern end of the port, you can climb the 192 steps up the Tour de l'Horloge (clock-tower) for views of the waterfront.

More to See

CHÂTEAU RAMEZAY

French governors, British conquerors and American generals have all stayed in this relic of the French regime. With its squat round towers and its rough stone finish, Château Ramezay is just like a piece of Normandy in North America.

One of north America's most venerable buildings, this Norman-style country house was commissioned in 1705 by Claude de Ramezay, 11th Governor of Montréal, and was the work of master mason Pierre Couturier, one of the leading architects of his day (the distinctive round tower was a 19th-century addition).

In 1745 de Ramezay's heir sold the property to governors of the Compagnie des Indes (West Indies Company), a fur-trading company that had the monopoly on beaver pelts sold in French North America until the coming of the British. Under the French the house became Montréal's most fashionable meeting place.

After 1763 the building became home to the Governors General of British North America (1764–1849), and during the brief American invasion of 1775 served as a military headquarters for American commanders Benedict Arnold and Richard Montgomery. Benjamin Franklin was here later the same year, engaged in a doomed attempt to persuade Montréalers to join the US.

In 1895 the house was bought and turned into a museum, its interior fitted and furnished as it might have been in the 18th century with paintings, costumes and furniture. The kitchen, one of the most appealing parts of the house, is filled with period utensils, and the intricate carving of the wood-paneled Grande Salle is a tactile reminder of the opulence of 18th-century Montréal.

➕ G10 ✉ 280 rue Notre-Dame Est at rue Saint-Claude
☎ 514/861–3708 🕐 Jun–Sep daily 10–6; Oct–May Tue–Sun 10–4.30
🚇 Champ-de-Mars 🚌 38
💰 Moderate

Strolling around Vieux-Port after sunset with twinkling lights reflecting in the water

HABITAT '67

Habitat '67 is a modern housing development designed for Expo '67 by Moshe Safdie, one of Montréal's leading architects. Safdie was disillusioned with suburbia and most public housing, especially high-rise developments, which he felt cut people off from open spaces, the amenities of the city and was ill-suited to families with growing children. His project here represented an attempt to build better housing more cheaply by mass-producing much of each housing unit in factories and then delivering them already made to the buildings' site. The project cost over $22 million—enough, at the time, to build up to eight ordinary townhouses. Today, from afar, the project, with its cubist house stacked on top of one another, looks strange and impressive—like Indian pueblos or an African medina—but Montréalers never really took to the dull concrete exteriors and inadequately protected pedestrian streets.

🚹 H12 ✉ Avenue Pierre-Dupuy, Cité du Havre 🚇 Place d'Armes

LABYRINTHE DU HANGAR 16

www.labyrintheduhangar16.com
A weather-protected maze with a new theme every year.

🚹 G10 ✉ Quai de L'Horloge, Vieux-Port
☎ 514/400–0099 🕐 Mid-May to mid-Jun, end Aug–end Sep daily 11.30–5.30; Jun 22–Aug 25 11–9 🚇 Champ-de-Mars
💰 Expensive

MAISON PAPINEAU

This beautiful building was originally built by John Campbell, a colonel in the British army, who is said to have purchased the land from Joseph Papineau, the grandfather of Louis-Joseph Papineau (1786–1871), one of the great political figures in the French-Canadian nationalist movement. In a rather strange twist, Campbell's widow sold the house to Louis-Joseph's father. He then in turn left it to Louis-Joseph, and it remained in the family until 1964. Today, it is owned by the Canadian government. The house has been lovingly restored to its splendid 1830s appearance as a memorial to Papineau; two stories

The strange box-like construction (Habitat '67) built for the Expo '67

having been carefully removed—along with 19 layers of wallpaper that had accumulated on the walls of the interior.

⊞ G10   ✉ 440 rue Bonsecours   ☎ None
🕐 Exterior only   🚇 Champ-de-Mars   ♿ On a sloping, cobbled street

MAISON PIERRE-DU-CALVET

A fine 18th-century house built in 1770 for Huguenot merchant Pierre du Calvet. Note the thick walls and fireplaces, the windows with little squares of glass imported from France, and the S-shape brackets on the facade.

⊞ G10   ✉ 401 rue Bonsecours
☎ 514/282–1725   🚇 Champ-de-Mars

MUSÉE MARC-AURÈLE FORTIN

Self-taught Québec artist Marc-Aurèle Fortin (1888–1970) set out to create a whole new style of landscape painting, and was particularly fond of using massive trees as his subject.

⊞ F12   ✉ 118 rue Saint-Pierre
☎ 514/845–6108   🕐 Tue–Sun 11–5
🚇 Square-Victoria (exit rue Saint-Jacques)

📟 61 (57 peak hours)   ♿ Poor: 8 steps to main entrance   🚻 Moderate

PLACE JACQUES-CARTIER

Right in the heart of Vieux-Montréal, this lovely cobbled square was created in 1804 as a municipal market; now its cafés, musicians, restaurants and quaint shops draw lively summer crowds. Nelson's Column is here and there are several fine 19th-century houses, including Maison del Vecchio, Maison Cartier and Maison Vandelac.

⊞ G11   🚇 Champ-de-Mars

PLACE ROYALE

Place Royale is Montréal's oldest square, and has an ancient history that stretches back to when the area's aboriginal population had an encampment on the site. Artifacts recovered locally suggest the area has been continually inhabited for at least 2,000 years. Between 1642 and 1676 the site had a transitional use, having been used as the site of an annual fur-trading market, when indigenous hunters would bring their

A bust of the explorer Jacques Cartier (left) sited in place Jacques-Cartier (right)

pelts to trade with French merchants. Thus was born the fur-trading industry that would be the basis of Montréal's wealth for decades to come. In 1701, the French and aboriginal peoples signed a treaty here (the spot is marked by the raised platform) that brought an end to the wars between them. In later years the square was the site of duels, whippings, public hangings and a market, and was known for a time as Customs Square. It took its present name in 1892.
➕ F11 ⓜ Place-d'Armes

PLACE D'YOUVILLE
This Vieux-Port square, very pleasant when not full of cars, was landscaped over a dried-up creek during the 19th century. It housed a fish market at one stage.
➕ F12 ⓜ Square-Victoria

RUE BONSECOURS
A good example of the classical ideals of Montréal's early French planners, with fine homes. Look for No. 401 Maison Pierre-du-Calvet and No. 440

Maison Papineau (both ▷ 36–37).
➕ G10 ⓜ Champ-de-Mars

RUE SAINT-AMABLE
This narrow and lively cobbled alley off Place Jacques-Cartier is notorious for the many portrait artists vying for business amid the summer throng.
➕ G11 ⓜ Place-d'Armes

RUE SAINT-PAUL
A block back from the waterfront, this is one of the city's oldest and most fashionable streets, with rather expensive cafés, restaurants and fascinating specialist shops.
➕ F12 ⓜ Place-d'Armes, Champ-de-Mars

VIEUX PALAIS DE JUSTICE
This impressive neoclassical courthouse, built in 1856, was used for almost a century to hear civil cases. Most of it is now used for municipal offices, but you can still admire the dome, exterior columns and impressive portico.
➕ F10 ✉ 155 rue Notre-Dame Est ⓜ Champ-de-Mars

Taking time to explore interesting specialist shops on Rue Saint-Paul

Vieux-Montréal

This easy walk takes you along the main streets and past the key churches, monuments, squares and civic buildings of Old Montréal.

DISTANCE: 3km (2 miles) **ALLOW:** 2–6 hours depending on sights visited

START

PLACE JACQUES-CARTIER ▷ 37
🚇 Place Jacques-Cartier 🚇 Champ-de-Mars

① Start at the northern end of Jacques-Cartier and walk east along rue Notre-Dame Est, passing Admiral Lord Horatio Nelson's monument.

② Continue on rue Notre-Dame Est past the Vieux Palais de Justice (▷ 38) and Hôtel de Ville on the left. Visit the Château Ramezay (▷ 35) on the right and the Lieu Historique National de Sir G.-É Cartier (▷ 29).

③ Turn right on rue Berri and right again on rue Saint-Paul Est, Vieux-Montréal's curving main street.

④ Pass the Maison Pierre-du-Calvet (▷ 37) on the right and Chapelle Notre-Dame-de-Bonsecours (▷ 28) and Marché Bonsecours (▷ 30) on the left. At Place Jacques-Cartier at the top go left on rue Notre-Dame Est.

END

PLACE JACQUES-CARTIER

⑧ Turn left on rue de la Commune Ouest to visit the Musée d'Archéologie d'Histoire (▷ 32). Continue along the waterfront until you reach the southern end of Place Jacques-Cartier.

⑦ Visit the Centre d'Histoire de Montréal (▷ 27) and, if you have time, the nearby Youville Stables (Écuries d'Youville) and Musée Marc-Aurèle Fortin (▷ 37). From the Musée Marc-Aurèle Fortin walk the short distance to the waterfront area.

⑥ After the Séminaire de Saint-Sulpice turn left down rue Saint-François-Xavier, past the Old Stock Exchange (now the Centaur Theatre). Go right on rue Saint-Paul Ouest and left on rue Saint-Pierre to Place d'Youville (▷ 38).

⑤ Pass the Palais de Justice (▷ 38) to the Basilique Notre-Dame (▷ 24).

Shopping

BOUTIQUE DES MÉTIERS D'ART DU QUÉBEC

www.metiers-d-art.qc.ca
This Marché Bonsecours outlet is a treasure house of beautiful craft, artisan and other design objects. The beautiful selection includes glass, ceramics, items crafted out of wood and jewlry, from the studios of 100 craftspeople based across the province.

➕ G10 ✉ 350 rue Saint-Paul Est ☎ 514/878–2787 Ⓜ Champ-de-Mars

CANADIAN MAPLE DELIGHTS

www.mapledelights.com
Mouthwatering aromas are overwhelming in this attractive shop and bistro, where you can sample or buy a wide range of maple syrup-based products, including superb pastries and delicious ice creams.

➕ G11 ✉ 84 rue Saint-Paul Est ☎ 514/765–3456 Ext 224 Ⓜ Champ-de-Mars

DESMARAIS ET ROBITAILLE

www.desmarais-robitaille.com
A unique store, Desmarais et Robitaille is worth a visit even if you don't intend to buy, for it stocks a wide range of fascinating religious and liturgical items for Montréal's clergy—anything from rosaries to a cardinal's ruf. But also religious and other interesting craft items might catch your eye.

➕ F11 ✉ 60 rue Notre-Dame Ouest ☎ 514/845–3194 Ⓜ Place-d'Armes

L'EMPREINTE COOPÉRATIVE

A dazzling store that showcases the work of numerous craftspeople from across the province of Québec.

➕ G10 ✉ 272 rue Saint-Paul Est ☎ 514/861–4427 Ⓜ Champs-de-Mars

GALERIE ART & CULTURE

The prices may be beyond you, but it is still great fun to admire the fine topographical and other 19th- and 20th-century paintings and artworks in this major gallery.

➕ G11 ✉ 227 rue Saint-Paul Ouest ☎ 514/843–5980 Ⓜ Place-d'Armes

---

SWEET SOUVENIRS

If you're looking for a "typical" souvenir to take home think maple. Québec produces more than two-thirds of the world's supply of maple syrup so, not surprisingly, the stuff is ubiquitous on Montréal breakfast tables, and confectionery, butter and sugar made from maple sap are common treats. The best time to buy is in spring when the supply is plentiful. Best prices are at farmers' markets.

GALERIE DES ARTS RELAIS DES ÉPOQUES

www.galerieartetculture.com
Montréal's flourishing contemporary art scene boasts this fine galley; a good place to view works by modern local artists.

➕ G10 ✉ 234 rue Saint-Paul Est ☎ 514/844–2133 Ⓜ Champs-de-Mars

GALERIE LE CHARIOT

www.galeriedechariot.com
Galleries of Inuit and other aboriginal art are increasingly popular and one of the most distinctive and purely Canadian of souvenirs. This one has one of Canada's largest collections of soapstone, ivory, jade and other Inuit carvings, as well as numerous other high-quality works of art. Prices, though, are correspondingly high.

➕ F11 ✉ 446 place Jacques-Cartier ☎ 514/875–6134 🚌 38 Ⓜ Champ-de-Mars

GRIFF 3000

This outlet in the Marché Bonsecours provides a quirky retail stage for a broad spectrum of fashion designers from around the city and across Québec in general. Items include men's, women's and children's clothes, plus hats and other accessories.

➕ G10 ✉ 350 rue Saint-Paul Est ☎ 514/398–0761 Ⓜ Champs-de-Mars

LA GUILDE GRAPHIQUE

www.guildegraphique.com
Come here for an impressive array of prints, engravings and etchings from different eras and in different styles and genres. An excellent place to browse for gifts to take home.

🕂 G11 ✉ 9 rue Saint-Paul Est ☎ 514/844–3438
Ⓜ Champ-de-Mars

L'INSTITUT DE DESIGN

www.idm.qc.ca
The store of Montréal's Institute of Design is based in the Marché Bonsecours, and sells all manner of interesting homeware and other items that are remarkable in some way for their innovative or eye-catching design.

🕂 G10 ✉ 390 rue Saint-Paul Est ☎ 514/866–2436
Ⓜ Champ-de-Mars

MARCHÉ BONSECOURS

www.marchebonsecours.qc.ca
The Marché Bonsecours is one of the most graceful buildings in Vieux-Montréal. Boutiques showcase local fashion, repro-antiques and Canadian crafts. Of particular interest are the toys and gizmos for home and office by the Institut de Design Montréal (see also individual entries).

🕂 G10 ✉ Rue Saint-Paul Street Est ☎ 514/872–7730
Ⓒ Sep–late Jun Sat–Wed

10–6, Thu, Fri 10–9; late Jun–Aug daily 10–9
Ⓜ Champ-de-Mars

POINTE-À-CALLIÈRE

www.pacmuseum.qc.ca
Vieux-Montréal is littered with second-rate souvenir stores unashamedly aimed at visitors, but for a superior memento of the city visit this museum gift shop in the Ancienne-Douane Building. It has a good selection of books on art and local history and archaeology, pieces of First Nations art, craft items and reproduction artefacts from Québec and around the world.

🕂 G11 ✉ 150 rue Saint-Paul Ouest ☎ 514/872–9149
Ⓜ Place-d'Armes

RUE SAINT-JACQUES

Rue Saint-Jacques between rue McGill in the west and boulevard Saint-Laurent is especially good for mid-price clothes stores for men and

---

MUSICAL SOUVENIRS

For something tonier, consider music. Because of its linguistic isolation, Québec has produced a rich popular culture of its own that's better known in France than in the US or even the rest of Canada. Try Archambault for the latest hits, or look for recordings by chansonniers Gilles Vigneault and Félix Leclerc or seminal rock musician Robert Charlebois.

---

women, and for its choice of shoe shops. Much the same goes for the stretch of rue Notre-Dame Ouest one block to the south.

🕂 F11 ✉ Rue Saint-Jacques
Ⓜ Place-d'Armes

RUE SAINT-PAUL

This street has a wide variety of stores, but is especially worth visiting for its many art galleries and craft shops. Most sell work by local and other Québécois artists and craftspeople, in a wide variety of styles. Even if you don't intend to buy, the quality of the items on sale make it worth looking into the galleries.

🕂 G10–11 ✉ Rue Saint-Paul
Ⓜ Champ-de-Mars

STEVE'S MUSIC STORE

www.stevemusic.com
This large, rambling store on the fringes of Vieux-Montréal is a magnet for musicians of every stripe, offering instruments, sheet music, songbooks and all manner of musical accessories.

🕂 F11 ✉ 51 Saint-Antoine Ouest ☎ 514/878–2216
Ⓜ Place-d'Armes

WORN DOORSTEP

www.theworndoorstep.com
The finest collection of quality Canadian souvenirs at this Marché Bonsecours store.

🕂 G10 ✉ 350 rue Saint-Paul ☎ 514/397–0666
Ⓒ Sat–Wed 10–6, Thu–Fri 10–9 Ⓜ Champ-de-Mars

Entertainment and Nightlife

AU CÉPAGE

Professionals and journalists keep the place lively with talk and debate all week. Good food, too.
🔲 F11 ✉ 212 rue Notre-Dame Ouest ☎ 514/845–5436 🕐 Daily noon–2am 🚇 Place d'Armes

LE CABARET DU ROY

www.oyez.ca
This restaurant and cabaret won't be to all tastes, as the music, costume, food and comedy all have an historic "New France" theme. You're served by "characters" from the Middle Ages. Most of the week it is only open to booked groups of 25 or more, but it opens normally on Friday and Saturday.
🔲 G10 ✉ 363 rue de la Commune Est ☎ 514/907–9000 🕐 Fri–Sat from 6.30pm. Terrace daily 11.30am–10pm 🚇 Champ-de-Mars

CENTAUR THEATRE

www.centaurtheatre.com
The city's foremost English-language theater has a grand setting in the city's former Stock Exchange Building.
🔲 F11 ✉ 453 rue Saint-François-Xavier ☎ 514/288–3161 🚇 Place d'Armes

CLUNY ARTBAR

On the fringes of the Vieux-Port, in an up-and-coming area, the Cluny ArtBar occupies part of a former foundry, otherwise mostly given over to large exhibition spaces. You can drink and order light lunches and sandwiches, plus more substantial dinners on some nights.
🔲 F12 ✉ 257 rue Prince, near rue Ottawa
☎ 514/866–1213 🕐 Mon–Fri 11am–2pm, Thu–Fri 6–9pm 🚇 Square Victoria

LES DEUX PIERROTS

www.lespierrots.com
A crowded and convivial Vieux-Montréal venue devoted to traditional Québécois folk music. Performances are on the terrace in fine weather.
🔲 G11 ✉ 104 rue Saint-Paul Est ☎ 514/861–1270 🕐 Mon–Fri 9am–6pm 🚇 Place-d'Armes

MODAVIE

www.modavie.com
The restaurant here is good for Mediterranean and other standards, but most people come for

CIRQUE DE SOLEIL

This circus has come a long way since it was founded by a handful of street performers on Montréal's Old Port waterfront in 1984. Its dance, acrobatics, costumes and drama has made it an international success. It has resident companies in Las Vegas and elsewhere, but not in Montréal, where it usually only performs in odd-numbered years in its blue-and-yellow tents on the Vieux-Port quayside ☎ 514/790–1245; www.cirquedusoleil.com

the large central bar, and for the live jazz, for which there is no cover charge. There's a good choice of malts and cigars, and bar snacks are free during happy hour on weekdays.
🔲 G11 ✉ 1 rue Saint-Paul Ouest ☎ 514/287–9582 🕐 Sun–Thu 11–11, Fri–Sat noon–3am (12–12 in winter); live jazz Sun–Thu 7pm–11pm, Fri–Sat 7pm–2am 🚇 Champ-de-Mars

PUB ST-PAUL

www.pubstpaul.com
The chief charms of this airy and friendly pub, with its rustic brick walls, flagstone floors and wooden beams, are its position close to the river and the views over the waterfront. On one of the area's most charming cobbled streets, it offers reasonable food, a wide range of beers and live music Friday and Saturday night.
🔲 G11 ✉ 124 rue Saint-Paul Est ☎ 514/874–0485 🕐 Mon–Thu 11am–1am, Fri–Sat 11am–3am 🚇 Champ-de-Mars, Place-d'Armes

TERRASSES BONSECOURS

www.terrassesbonsecours.com
Three terraces, an indoor bistro and an outdoor "amphitheater" area, plus, as well as a normal bar, there is a "water bar" that offers a choice of mineral waters.
🔲 G10 ✉ Quai de l'Horloge ☎ 514/288–9407 🕐 Jun–end Sep daily 11am–1am 🚇 Champ-de-Mars

Restaurants

PRICES

Prices are approximate, based on a 3-course meal for one person.

$$$	over $40
$$	$20–$40
$	under $20

AIX CUISINE DU TERROIR ($$$)

www.aixcuisine.com

This chic and intimate restaurant complements the contemporary look of the hotel in which it is housed. Modern French cooking and you can eat from a bar menu in the bar, Suite 701.

🚩 F11 ☒ Hôtel Le Place-d'Armes, 711 Côte de la place-d'Armes ☎ 514/904–1201 or 888/450–1887 🕐 Lunch Mon–Fri, dinner daily. Bar and lounge daily 11am–11pm 🚇 Place-d'Armes

À L'AVENTURE ($$)

www.alaventure.com

A busy and long-established restaurant on the area's main square, with a large bar, bistro and dining room. Good for a quick meal or drink, especially in the summer, when you can sit on the outside terrace.

🚩 G10 ☒ 438 place Jacques-Cartier ☎ 514/866–9439 🕐 Daily lunch, dinner 🚇 Place-d'Armes

AUBERGE LE SAINT-GABRIEL ($$)

www.auberge1754.com

This characterful inn was founded in 1754 and is said to be the oldest in North America. The dining rooms are large with seating on the terrace and the setting is suitably venerable, with a lovely fireplace and comforting French and Québécois cooking.

🚩 G11 ☒ rue Saint-Gabriel ☎ 514/878–3561 🕐 Daily lunch, dinner Apr–Aug; closed Sat–Mon for lunch and Sun–Mon for dinner rest of year 🚇 Place-d'Armes

BONAPARTE ($$$)

www.bonaparte.ca

Sit in the fireplace room overlooking rue Saint-Sacrement and you'll swear you're in Paris. The food is French, too.

🚩 F11 ☒ 443 rue Saint-François-Xavier ☎ 514/844–4368 🕐 Mon–Fri lunch, dinner, Sat, Sun dinner 🚇 Place d'Armes

BORIS BISTRO ($$)

www.borisbistro.com

ETHNIC FLAVORS

French cuisine dominates Montréal's dining scene. More than 30 different ethnic groups are represented in Montréal. Greek and Italian immigrants have established an enduring place in Montréalers' stomachs. Cantonese cooking has been a presence since the late 1800s. Refugees from Indochina in the 1970s opened Vietnamese restaurants and noodle shops. The current craze is for Thai food.

French bistro food such homemade sausage, braised rabbit—served on a delightful tree-shaded terrace in Vieux-Montréal.

🚩 F12 ☒ 443 rue McGill ☎ 514/848–9575 🕐 May–Sep daily lunch, dinner; Oct–Apr lunch Mon–Fri, dinner Tue–Sat 🚇 Square Victoria

LE BOURLINGUEUR ($$)

Fish and seafood are the main here, though non seafood options are also available. Try the poached salmon, the house specialty.

🚩 F11 ☒ 363 rue Saint-François-Xavier ☎ 514/845–3646 🕐 Daily lunch, dinner; closed Sat lunch Nov–end Mar 🚇 Place-d'Armes

CAFÉ DU CHÂTEAU ($)

A delightful café in the gardens of the Château Ramezay, offering a short but tasty lunch menu of salads, sandwiches and hot and cold drinks.

🚩 G12 ☒ 280 rue Notre-Dame Est ☎ 514/861–3708 🕐 Lunch daily (closes at 4pm) May–end Sep 🚇 Champ-de-Mars

CAFÉ STASH ($$)

Here you sit on pews to consume robust and warming Polish dishes—hot borscht, pierogi and several kinds of sausage.

🚩 G11 ☒ 200 rue Saint-Paul Ouest ☎ 514/845–6611 🕐 Daily lunch, dinner 🚇 Place d'Armes

CHEZ L'ÉPICIER ($$$)

Fresh market cuisine served in the surroundings of an old grocery store offers unusual variations on French cuisine. Try the sweetbreads braised in apple juice and fresh thyme, or the salmon stew with salsify.

✚ G10 ✉ 311 rue Saint-Paul ☎ 514/878–2232 🕓 Dinner daily, lunch Mon–Fri 🚇 Champ-de-Mars

CLAUDE POSTEL ($)

Chic café in Vieux-Montréal; chocolates, pastries and first-class sandwiches, as well as hot lunches. The fixed-price menues are good value. In summer sample decadently rich *gelato*.

✚ F11 ✉ 75 rue Notre-Dame Ouest ☎ 514/844–8750 🕓 Daily lunch 🚇 Place d'Armes

CUBE ($$$)

Super trendy restaurant in the boutique Hôtel Saint-Paul serves bold, market cuisine. The wine list is excellent. Minimalist decor; fashionable crowd.

✚ F12 ✉ 355 rue McGill ☎ 514/876–2823 🕓 Mon–Fri lunch, dinner, Sat, Sun dinner 🚇 Square Victoria

DA EMMA ($$)

Stone-walled basement room, with pillars and wooden beams, near the Vieux-Port. The cuisine is Italian; try fettucine with porcini mushrooms or roast baby pig.

✚ G12 ✉ 777 rue de la Commune Ouest ☎ 514/392–1568 🕓 Mon–Fri lunch, dinner, Sat dinner 🚇 Square Victoria

EGGSPECTATION ($)

www.eggspectation.ca
Part of a small chain, but none the worse for that. Very popular, and excellent for snacks and light meals in a fun atmosphere.

✚ F11 ✉ 201 rue Saint-Jacques ☎ 514/282–0119 🕓 Lunch Mon–Sat 🚇 Place-d'Armes

GANDHI ($)

Alternatives to French and Italian cuisine are rare in the Vieux-Port area, so this modern Indian restaurant, with crisp white napery and smart bare wood floors, makes a pleasant change. None of the food is too heavily spiced, and there are plenty of good vegetarian options.

✚ G11 ✉ 230 rue Saint-Paul Ouest ☎ 514/845–5866 🕓 Dinner daily, lunch Mon–Fri 🚇 Place-d'Armes

NAGOYA ($$)

This is an ideal place to stop on a tour of Vieux-Montréal. Grilled, spicy beef, salmon, chicken and squid are served in lacquered boxes along with salad and sticky rice.

✚ F11 ✉ 140 rue Notre-Dame Ouest ☎ 514/845–5864 🕓 Mon–Sat lunch, dinner 🚇 Place d'Armes

OLIVE ET GOURMANDO ($)

www.oliveetgourmando.com
Superb bakery that offers salads, *panini* and delicious hot or cold sandwiches with generous and often exotic fillings. Perfect for a snack at any time of the day.

✚ G11 ✉ 315 rue Saint-Paul Ouest ☎ 514/350–1083 🕓 Breakfast and lunch Tue–Sat until 6pm

TOQUE! ($$$)

Toque! has been one of Montréal's gastronomic temples for years, and its contemporary French and Asian fusion food has lost nothing over the time. First choice for a treat.

✚ F11 ✉ 900 place Jean-Paul-Riopelle, near rue saint-François-Xavier ☎ 514/499–2084 🕓 Daily dinner, lunch Mon–Fri 🚇 Place-d'Armes

---

SATISFYING FOOD

One of the hardest things to find in Montréal is the hearty Québécois food the French pioneers developed to help them survive harsh winters and hard-working summers—thick pea soup, spicy *tourtière* (a kind of meat pie), pigs' feet, game pie and meatball stew.

Try **Binerie Mont Royal** (✉ 367 avenue Mont-Royal Est ☎ 514/285-9078 🕓 Daily lunch, dinner Mon–Fri); and **Chez Clo** (✉ 3199 rue Ontario Est ☎ 514/522-5348 🕓 Daily lunch only

Lovely churches, venerable museums and peaceful squares sit beside glittering sky-scrapers, dramatic art galleries and busy shopping streets, while beneath is another world entirely, the Underground City.

⑩

⑪

⑫

⑬

C   D   E

138

Salle Wilfrid Pelletier
Théâtre du Nouveau Monde

Place-des-Arts
Place des Arts

Musée d'Art Contemporain

Complexe Desjardin

OUEST
Rue de la Concorde
Président-Kennedy
OUEST
R Balmoral
RUE
OUEST
DE
Jeanne-Mance
Le Spectrum
BLEURY

Rue Mayor
Rue City
Rue Église St-James
Rue Councillors
Rue Aylmer
Église St-James
Église du Gesù
St-Alexandre
Rue Dowd

SHERBROOKE
Avenue McGill
Avenue Victoria
DE
RUE
BOULEVARD
La Baie
Union
STE-CATHERINE

Royal Victoria College

McCord Museum of Canadian History

Tour BNP-Banque Laurentienne

Christ Church Cathedral

Maison de la Poste

Square Phillips

Place Phillips

St Patrick's Basilica

Champs du Beaver

Avenue McGill College

RUE

Ave McGill

College

UNIVERSITY

Ave-Union

RENÉ-LÉVESQUE

Rue Ste-Catherine

Rue Cathcart

Place Ville-Marie

Underground City

Rue Belmont

Square Victor

La Tour Bell

Bell Canada

de la Gauchetière

𝒕

Metcalfe

Édifice Sunlife

BOULEVARD

Mansfield

GARE CENTRALE

Square Dorchester

112

Rue Stanley

Rue Drummond

Cathédrale Marie-Reine-du-Monde

RUE

Bonaventure

Place Bonaventure

1000 de la Gauchetière

Édifice IBM-Marathon

PEEL

Rue de la Cathédrale

Rue de la

Postes Canada

GARE WINDSOR

Planétarium de Montréal

0   250 m
0   250 yds

The huge copper cupola (left) and intricate statues atop the Cathédrale (right)

Cathédrale Marie-Reine-du-Monde

Mary Queen of the World Cathedral brings a taste of the Italian Renaissance into the heart of Montréal. Dwarfed now by skyscrapers, the cathedral was a daring monument to 19th-century Roman Catholic triumphalism.

St. Peter's in miniature Bishop Ignace Bourget, who began the cathedral three years after Canadian confederation, intended to underline papal supremacy and show that Catholicism still dominated what was then the largest city in the Dominion. So he set the cathedral, a one-quarter-size replica of St. Peter's in Rome, at the heart of the city's Anglo-Protestant district. Begun in 1870, the building was completed in 1894.

Step inside In contrast to the lovely intimacy of Notre-Dame in Vieux-Montréal, the interior is somber, although the interiors of both churches are the work of architect Victor Bourgeau. The gloom was intended to intensify the effect of candles and accentuate the rose windows. The opulent high altar features a copy of the vast *baldacchino*, or altar canopy, by Bernini in St. Peter's, while the first little chapel in the left aisle has a red-flocked sanctuary filled with medals and saintly relics. Bishop Bourget is interred in a second chapel on the same side of the church, his recumbent figure surrounded by the tombs of his successors. On a pillar facing the bishop's tomb is a memorial to the men from the diocese who served in the Papal Zouaves in the fight against Italian nationalists.

HIGHLIGHTS

- Stained glass
- High altar
- Bourget Chapel

Christ Church Cathedral

The gabled facade of the Gothic cathedral enhanced by a slender spire

THE BASICS

www.montreal.anglican.
org/cathedral

🕀 E11

✉ 635 rue Sainte-
Catherine Ouest and 1444
avenue Union

☎ Cathedral staff
514/843–6577

🕐 Daily 8–6

🚇 McGill

♿ Very good; ramps from
street

💷 Free

❓ Midday and evening
choral and organ concerts

HIGHLIGHTS

● Choral Evensong (4pm
daily)
● Nave altar
● Carved angels in the
Chapterhouse
● Coventry Cross
● Bishop's Throne
● Chapel of St. John
● Pulpit

The seat of Montréal's Anglican bishop is a graceful ship of serenity floating (almost literally) on a sea of commerce. There are department stores on either side of it, a skyscraper behind, and a shopping mall right underneath.

Copy This beautifully simple church is the city's Anglican cathedral, built between 1857 and 1859 at the instigation of Francis Fulford, Montréal's first Anglican bishop. Its neo-Gothic style is reminiscent of a 14th-century English church, but its plan is actually a straight copy of the Anglican cathedral in Fredericton, N. B., which was designed by the same architect, Frank Wills. The steeple had problems, proving to be too heavy for the soft, unstable ground and was replaced in 1927 with one made of aluminum plates, doctored to match the stone of the rest of the church. Among the notable objects inside the church is a cross (left and above the pulpit) made from nails rescued from the bombed Coventry Cathedral in England.

Money matters Over time soaring towers have dwarfed the cathedral, while high maintenance costs and dwindling congregations led to a budgetary shortfall. The Anglican authorities found an imaginative solution in 1985 when they leased the land around and beneath the cathedral to developers. The church now sits atop Les Promenades de la Cathédrale, a busy mall. Shoppers, office workers and store clerks of all faiths retreat to the cathedral at midday for free concerts and organ recitals.

The building is contemporary (right), as are the sculptures and paintings inside (left)

Musée d'Art Contemporain

Montréal boasts one of Canada's most important museums of contemporary art. The stark, modern building is impressive, from its offbeat doors to the distinctive angular galleries and central atrium.

On the Move Founded in 1964 by the Québec government, the museum occupied three different buildings before moving into its present home, a superb plain-faced modern building only a stone's throw from Place des Arts, in 1992. It originally focused on the work of indigenous Québécois artists, but the museum has increasingly widened its scope and mounts temporary exhibitions by artists from around the world.

The paintings Works in the gallery date from around 1939 up to the present, with at least 60 per cent of the more than 5,000 works of art in the museum's collection of Québécois artists. Among those represented are David Moore, Alfred Pellan, Jean-Paul Riopelle, with 75 paintings by Montréal artist Paul-Émile Borduas. Other Canadian artists include Jack Bush, Michael Snow and Barbara Steinman. Works by Picasso, Lichtenstein and Warhol are also on display. There is a growing video art collection. Much of the permanent collection is often moved out to make way for temporary exhibitions, such as retrospectives of the work of Guido Molinari, one of Canada's leading abstract artists, and Henry Saxe, one of the country's foremost sculptors, and exhibitions of recent acquisitions. Remember to look round the sculpture garden.

THE BASICS

🚩 E10
✉ 185 rue Sainte-Catherine Ouest at rue Jeanne-Mance
☎ 514/847–6226 or 514/847–6253
🕐 Tue, Thu–Sun 11–6, Wed 11–9 (also Mon 11–6 mid-May to early Sep)
🍴 La Rotonde restaurant (lunch, dinner)
🚇 Place-des-Arts
🚌 15, 55, 80, 129, 535
♿ Very good
💰 Expensive; free Wed from 6pm for collection; reduced rate for exhibitions
❓ Guided tours, weekend schedule and child activities

HIGHLIGHTS

● Architecture
● *Lips*, Geneviève Cadieux
● Steel atrium
● Sculpture garden
● *L'Île fortifiée*, Paul-Émile Borduas

McCord Museum of Canadian History

HIGHLIGHTS

- Notman Photographic Archives
- Stuffed elephant
- Caricatures
- Historic prints and maps
- Decorative arts collection
- Guided tours

TIPS

- Creative workshops and day camps are available.
- Call for details of guided tours ($9) or pick up an audio tour ($8).

One of Canada's best museums, the McCord Museum of Canadian History possesses a huge range of objects including Native Canadian culture and an important photographic collection, offering an insight into Montréal's past.

Bigger and bigger   Montréal lawyer David Ross McCord (1844–1930), the scion of a prosperous Scots-Irish family, was a collector with an insatiable appetite for anything connected with Canadian history. In the 1920s he gave his huge collection of books, furniture, clothing, guns, paintings, documents, toys and photographs to McGill University, where it was housed in the McGill Union Building (1906). A $20-million renovation in 1992 doubled the museum's size, but still there is space to display only a fragment of the 1,375,000 items.

An Inuit totem pole (far left), Indian garments (bottom middle) and headdress (right)
all on display inside the McCord Museum of Canadian History (top middle)

Photographs collection The museum is
strongest on the culture and history of Native
Canadians, and devotes several galleries to aboriginal furs, carvings and embroidered beadwork. The
collections also include some 10,000 costumes,
many dating from the 18th century and earlier. Also
remarkable are the Notman Photographic Archives,
a collection of prints and glass prints produced by
photographic pioneer William Notman, who captured Victorian life in Montréal. The photographs
include formal balls, soldiers marching and mem-
bers of the exclusive Montréal Athletic Association
in snowshoes. Each of the hundreds of people
shown in these pictures was photographed individ-
ually in the studio and then the photos mounted
on to an appropriate background. In all there are
450,000 photographs in the Archives, plus
800,000 images taken by other photographers.

THE BASICS

www.musee-mccord.qc.ca
🔠 D11
✉ 690 rue Sherbrooke
Ouest at rue Victoria
☎ 514/398–7100
🕐 Mon and hols 10–6,
Tue–Fri 10–6, Sat, Sun
10–5. Closed Mon in win-
ter except public hols
🍴 The McCord Café
Ⓜ McGill
🚌 24, 125
♿ Good
💷 Expensive (free Sat
10–12)
❓ Guided tours, reading
room

St. Patrick's Basilica

HIGHLIGHTS

● Pulpit
● Sanctuary lamp
● Darcy McGee's pew

TIPS

● Take a break in the pleasant garden space on the west side of the basilica.
● Hear the St. Patrick Basilica choir during the celebration of the Eucharist at 11am September to June.
● Mass is sung in Latin every third Sunday of the month September to June at 11am.

Visitors arrive by the busload to see the Basilique Notre-Dame-de-Montréal. Just a few blocks north, the pious and the knowledgeable have the delicate gold and green beauty of St. Patrick's Basilica to themselves.

Our church Bishop Ignace Bourget gave only grudging approval when the Irish Catholics asked for a church of their own in 1843. The Mass, he reasoned, was in Latin, and most of the Irish spoke Gaelic at home. Surely they could go to church with their French-speaking brethren. But the Irish persisted and with help from the Sulpician priests erected a graceful neo-Gothic church.

Then there was light On sunny afternoons, light floods through the stained-glass figures of the four

After appreciating St. Patrick's Basilica from the outside (left), be sure to venture inside to see the real beauty of this place, particularly with the sun flooding through the stained-glass windows (right)

Evangelists, and fills the soaring nave with a honey-color glow. The vault over the sanctuary gleams with green-and-gold mosaics and the air smells of beeswax polish and incense. The pulpit is decorated with panels of the 12 Apostles, a huge sanctuary lamp is graced with a half-dozen 2m (6ft) tall angels, and poet Emile Nelligan was baptized in the ornate font. But what is unusual is the presence of the communion of saints. Statues of bishops, martyrs, missionaries, princesses and peasants jostle for space on the main altar and crowd the niches of the side altars. Another 150 holy men and women are honored in painted panels that line the walls of the nave. One of the fathers of the confederation of Canada is remembered: Thomas Darcy McGee was buried in St. Patrick's after his assassination in 1868. His pew (No. 240) is marked with a Canadian flag.

THE BASICS

www.stpatricksmtl.ca

✚ E11

✉ 460 boulevard René-Lévesque Ouest

☎ 514/866–7379

🕐 Daily 8.30–6

Ⓜ McGill

♿ Fair

💲 Free

HIGHLIGHTS

● Place Ville Marie
● Les Halles de la Gare
● 1000 de la Gauchetière and ice rink
● Atrium of the ICAD Building
● Centre CPD Capital and Terrasse du Parquet

TIP

● Do not only explore the Underground City by day: 40 theaters, cinemas and other entertainment venues offer plenty to do in the evening.

It's possible to arrive in Montréal by train in winter and spend a pleasant week without once stepping outside. You could shop, dine, see an opera, go to church, or even watch a hockey game without putting on your coat.

Beginnings Montréal's vast Underground City (Cité Souterrain) began in the early 1960s, when a mall full of shops and boutiques opened underneath the main plaza of Place Ville-Marie, the city's first modern skyscraper. Both it and the neighboring Queen Elizabeth Hotel were built over the Canadian National Railway's tracks so it seemed natural enough to link both of them with Central Station, and to Place Bonaventure to the south. The idea caught on and really took off when the Métro opened in 1966.

Le Centre Eaton (left) and Place Montréal Trust (right), just two of the exciting retail attractions that make up Montréal's Underground City

Growth The underground now has more than 29km (18 miles) of wide, well-lighted tunnels, mostly clustered around 10 of the 64km (40-mile) Métro system's 65 stations. At last count, the system encompassed seven major hotels, two universities, both train stations, more than 1,700 boutiques, two department stores, more than 200 restaurants, at least 30 cinemas, the Olympic Stadium, and the Centre Bell. The only universities are French: the Université de Montréal and the Université du Québec à Montréal (UQAM). Oddly in a city that was once so Roman Catholic, the only church with its own link to the system is the Protestant Christ Church Cathedral. Remember that only the links are underground: most of the shops and malls are above ground. In fact, the soaring glass lobby of Place des Arts is as much a part of the system as the Métro stations.

THE BASICS

🔢 E12

✉ Access at Métro stations in center

🕐 Sun–Fri 5.30am–12.30am, Sat 5.30am–1am

🚇 Peel, McGill, Bonaventure, Place-des-Arts, Square-Victoria

♿ Fair

More to See

ALDRED BUILDING

The Aldred Building, or Édifice Prevoyance (1928), is celebrated for its interesting art deco features.

➕ F11 ✉ 501–507 place d'Armes
🚇 Place d'Armes

AVENUE MCGILL COLLEGE

This short wide boulevard runs from Cathcart near Place Ville-Marie up to McGill University's Roddick Gates. If you stand on the Place Ville-Marie plaza, you get a beautiful sweeping view of the mountains and the campus framed by glass office towers.

➕ D11 🚇 McGill

BANQUE DE MONTRÉAL

Canada's oldest financial institution, was founded in 1817. Thirty years later its headquarters moved to this neo-classical building inspired by Rome's Pantheon. The bank's small museum displays coins, mechanical piggy banks and a check written on a beaver pelt.

➕ F11 ✉ 119 rue Saint-Jacques
☎ 514/877–7373 🕐 Mon–Fri 9–3
🚇 Place-d'Armes ♿ Good 💷 Free

ÉDIFICE IBM-MARATHON

Designed in 1991 by New York's Kohn, Pederson, Fox, this glass-and-granite tower standing 47-stories high is one of Montréal's most innovative buildings.

➕ D12 ✉ 1250 boulevard René-Lévesque Ouest, between rues Stanley and Drummond
🚇 Bonaventure

PLACE D'ARMES

Place d'Armes was laid out at the end of the 17th century around the main source of drinking water for the city's first French settlement. In the center stands a statue (1895) of Paul de Chomedey, Montréal's founder, Sieur de Maisonneuve. Around it lie the Basilique Notre-Dame (▷ 24–25), Montréals' oldest building the Séminaire St-Sulpice, the Banque de Montréal, the 1930 art deco Aldred Building (▷ left), or Édifice Prevoyance, and the eight-story Édifice New York Life (1888). To the south are the waterfront and Vieux-Port attractions (▷ 34).

➕ F11 🚇 Place d'Armes

Many of the city's most distinguished buildings surround the Place d'Armes

PLANÉTARIUM DE MONTRÉAL

www.planetarium.montreal.qc.ca
Regular shows in the big domed theater offer guided tours to our solar system and more distant galaxies. Themed schedules alter every few months, exploring space collisions, black holes, sun spots, eclipses and the star that guided the Magi to Bethlehem.

➕ E13 ✉ 1000 rue Saint-Jacques Ouest ☎ 514/872–4530; 🕐 Late Jun–early Sep daily; early Sep–late Jun Tue–Sun (precise dates can vary year to year) 💲 Moderate

RUE SAINTE-CATHERINE

Montréal's premier shopping street, spoiled in places by fast-food joints, is at its most appealing between rues University and Peel, and within the area of rues de la Montagne, Crescent and Bishop.

➕ D12 🚇 Guy-Concordia

SQUARE-DORCHESTER

This major downtown green space is lined with churches, historic buildings and office buildings. Just off rue Sainte-Catherine (▷ left), it's popular in summer with visitors and city workers. The main Infotouriste tourist office is here.

➕ D12 🚇 Peel, Bonaventure

SQUARE PHILLIPS

An immense, pigeon-spattered statue of King Edward VII, sculpted by Philippe Hébert in 1914, dominates this pleasant open space on rue Sainte-Catherine in the middle of downtown. In summer street vendors' open stands are found at the king's feet, competing with the shops that surround the square. Across the street and slightly to the west is Christ Church Cathedral (▷ 50).

➕ E11 🚇 McGill

TOUR BNP-BANQUE LAURENTIENNE

These twin blue-glass towers are eye-catching on the downtown skyline, dominating a particularly pleasant stretch of avenue McGill.

➕ D11 ✉ 1981 avenue McGill College 🚇 McGill

The "Crowd" outside the BNP Tower
Under the stars at the Planetarium

Heart of Downtown

At street level this walk explores the dazzling high-rise heart of the modern city above the underground in the Cité Souterrain.

DISTANCE: 3km (2 miles) **ALLOW:** 1.5 hours

START

PLACE DES ARTS ▷ 57
🚇 Place-des-Arts 🏛 Musée d'Art Contemporain

END

SQUARE-DORCHESTER ▷ 59
🚇 Peel

1 Start on place des Arts at the Musée d'Art Contemporain (▷ 51), which houses Canada's finest collection of modern art.

2 Follow signs to rue Sainte-Catherine, stopping at Square Phillips (▷ 59) for the Anglican Christ Church Cathedral (▷ 50).

3 Continue along rue Sainte-Catherine. Turn right on avenue McGill College (▷ 58), an avenue, with views of Mont-Royal, that ends at the gates to the McGill University (▷ 70).

4 You can detour right for a block on rue Sherbrooke to visit the McCord Museum (▷ 52) at rue Victoria, or turn left and walk through part of the Square Mile.

8 Turn left on rue Saint-Marc, right on rue Sainte-Catherine and right again on rue Peel to finish your walk at Square-Dorchester.

7 Turn left on rue du Fort and left again on rue Baile to visit the Canadian Centre for Architecture (▷ 98).

6 As you continue you come to the Musée des Beaux-Arts (▷ 74) at the corner of avenue du Musée. Continue along Sherbrooke to the Grande Séminaire de Montréal at rue du Fort.

5 The Square Mile was once home to Canada's 19th-century plutocrats.

Shopping

LA BAIE (THE BAY)
www.hbc.com
This is the flagship department store of the Hudson's Bay Company, founded in 1891. It still sells the company's distinctive traditional blankets, as well as the full range of usual department store goods.
➕ E11 ✉ 585 rue Sainte-Catherine Ouest at Square Phillips ☎ 514/281–4422 Mon–Thu 9.30–7, Fri 9.30–9, Sat 8–5, Sun 10–5 🚇 McGill

BIRKS
www.birks.com
One of the country's most prestigious and longest-established jewelers, particularly known for its fine silverware and classy blue packaging. You'll also find high-quality china and crystal. Of the several city locations, this branch is particularly worth a visit just for a look at its wonderfully striking art deco interior.
➕ E11 ✉ 1240 Square Phillips ☎ 514/397–2511 🕐 Mon–Wed 10–6, Thu, Fri 10–9, Sat 9.30–5, Sun 12–5 🚇 McGill

BROWN CHAUSSURES
Fashionable and expensive men's and women's shoes, boots and bags. This popular chain has half a dozen outlets around the city.
➕ E12 ✉ 1 place Ville-Marie at rue University ☎ 514/861–8925 🕐 Mon–Wed 10–5, Thu, Fri 10–9, Sat 9–5, Sun 12–5 🚇 McGill, Bonaventure

LE CENTRE EATON
www.centreeatondemontreal.com
Ironically, the venerable Canadian department store that gave this mall its name closed its doors in 1999. But the mall—the largest in the downtown core with five floors of boutiques and shops—is still thriving.
➕ E12 ✉ 705 rue Sainte-Catherine Ouest ☎ 514/288–3708 🕐 Mon–Fri 10–9, Sat 10–5, Sun 12–5 🚇 McGill

CHAS JOHNSON & SONS
www.kiltsmontreal.com
This fine traditional tailor's shop, with three kilt makers on call, is one of the few places in Canada still offering made-to-measure Highland regalia. They also stock all the necessary Scottish

SHOPPING DISTRICTS
Montréal's best shopping is in the malls close to the McGill Métro station and along rue Sainte-Catherine. Cheaper shops abound in Vieux-Montréal. More Bohemian stores can be found around boulevard Saint-Laurent (The Main). Bookshops, galleries and antiques shops are in nearby rue Saint-Denis, while still other interesting options are springing up around avenue du Mont-Royal and rue Saint-Viateur.

extras—hose, sporrans, jackets, skeandhus—as well as a full line of men's wear.
➕ E11 ✉ 1184 place Philippe, near boulevard René-Lévesque ☎ 514/878–1931 🕐 Tue–Fri 9–5.30, Sat 9.30–4.30 🚇 McGill

COMPLEXE DESJARDINS
This vast multitiered complex is one of the largest malls in eastern downtown. In addition to about 100 shops you'll find restaurants and bistros, cinemas, offices and a large piazza used for cultural events. Fountains and exotic plants make the place very pleasant.
➕ E10 ✉ Rue Sainte-Catherine Ouest at Saint-Urbain ☎ 514/281–1870 🕐 Mon–Wed 9.30–6, Thu, Fri 9.30–9, Sat 9.30–5, Sun 12–5 🚇 Place-des-Arts

EDIFICE BELGO
This building is essentially a mall for art galleries, showing-casing established and upcoming artists. Some of the best include Troise Points and Optica Centre for Contemporary Art.
➕ E11 ✉ 372 rue Sainte-Catherine Ouest ☎ Troise Points 514/866–8008; Optica 514/874–1666 🕐 Wed–Fri 12–6, Sat 12–5 🚇 Place-des-Arts

HENRI HENRI
www.henrihenri.ca
If you want a hat—any

hat—then this is the shop. One of the best stores of its type in North America, it has everything from cheap baseball caps to $1,000 Homburgs and Panamas.

🔁 F10 ✉ 189 rue Sainte-Catherine Ouest, corner of rue Hôtel-de-Ville

☎ 514/288-0109 or 888/388-0109 🕐 Mon–Thu 10–6, Fri 10–9, Sat–Sun 10–5

🚇 Saint-Laurent

INDIGO

www.indigo.ca

This bright, airy branch of a Toronto-based chain has a café and a huge selection of books.

🔁 D11 ✉ 1500 avenue McGill ☎ 514/281-5549

🕐 Daily 9am–11pm

🚇 McGill

PARAGRAPHE BOOK STORE

www.paragraphbooks.com

Popular with serious book lovers and students. Lectures and readings by leading Canadian authors.

🔁 D11 ✉ 2220 avenue McGill College

☎ 514/845-5811 🕐 Mon–Fri 7am–11pm, Sat, Sun 9am–11pm 🚇 McGill

PETIT MUSÉE

www.petitmusee.com

Sensational antiques from around the world, at stratospheric prices. It's worth taking a look even if you don't intend to buy.

🔁 C12 ✉ 1494 rue Sherbrooke Ouest

☎ 514/937-6161 🕐 Tue–Sat 10–5 🚇 Guy-Concordia

PLACE VILLE-MARIE

This once-gloomy mall now provides a home for more than 100 retail outlets, many of them top designer boutiques.

🔁 E12 ✉ 1 place Ville-Marie

☎ 514/861-9393 🕐 Mon–Sat 9–6

🚇 Bonaventure

PROMENADES DE LA CATHÉDRALE

A popular place to stroll, the breathtaking Promenades are directly beneath Christ Church Cathedral.

🔁 E11 ✉ 625 rue Sainte-Catherine Ouest at rue University ☎ 514/849-9925

🕐 Mon–Wed 10–6, Thu, Fri 10–9, Sat 9–5, Sun 12–5

🚇 McGill

ROOTS

www.roots.com

Roots is a national institution, a sort of Canadian

MALL SHOPPING

The advantage of shopping in Montréal's state-of-the-art malls, is that it's an all-season endeavor. Most of them are linked into the Underground City's (▷ 56) extensive network of tunnels and Métro lines. Many of the city's major department stores are also connected to the system, and some of them have become minimalls, opening shops within shops to showcase designers such as Jean-Claude Chacok, Guy Laroche and Cacherel.

Gap, full of inexpensive and timeless classics.

🔁 D12 ✉ 1035 rue Sainte-Catherine Ouest

☎ 514/845-7995 🕐 Mid-Jun–end Aug Mon–Fri 10–9, Sat 9–5, Sun 11–5; Sep–mid-Jun Mon–Wed 10–6, Thu, Fri 10–9, Sat 9–5, Sun 11–5

🚇 Peel

SIMONS

www.simons.ca

Where La Baie is mostly traditional, Simons is a more youthful department store, with an emphasis on good, modern clothes for men and women.

🔁 D12 ✉ 977 rue Sainte-Catherine Ouest

☎ 514/282-1840

🕐 Mon–Wed 10–6, Thu–Fri 10–9, Sat 9.30–5, Sun 12–5

🚇 Peel

ULYSSES LA LIBRAIRIE DU VOYAGE

Travel books in French and English, as well as maps and assorted travel-related artifacts.

🔁 D11 ✉ 560 avenue du Président-Kennedy, near avenue Union

☎ 514/843-7222

🕐 Mon–Wed 10–6, Thu, Fri 10–8, Sat 10–5, Sun 12–5

🚇 McGill

THE WORD

An eccentric shop with books on philosophy, art and literature. Cash only.

🔁 D11 ✉ 469 rue Milton

☎ 514/845-5640

🕐 Mon–Wed 10–6, Thu–Fri 10–9, Sat 11–6 🚇 McGill

Entertainment and Nightlife

CAFÉ SARAJEVO

This eccentric little hang-out on the edge of Chinatown appeals to artists, students and local literati. Music on weekends ranges from blues to cabaret, all spiced up with a little belly dancing. Limited menu of eastern European food.

🚇 E10 ✉ 2080 rue Clark ☎ 514/284–5629 🕐 Tue–Thu 5pm–1am, Fri, Sat 5pm–3am 🚇 Saint-Laurent

CLUB 737

www.altitude737.com
On top of Place Ville-Marie, this is possibly the most elegant disco in town—it certainly has the best views.

🚇 E12 ✉ 1 place Ville-Marie ☎ 514/397–0737 🕐 Restaurant Tue–Fri lunch, dinner, Sat dinner. Club Thu–Sat, Mon 10pm–3am, winter Fri–Sat
🚇 Bonaventure, McGill

CLUB LOUNGE KARINA'S

One of the biggest and slickest clubs on trendy rue Crescent. A mix of live and recorded Latin, jazz, R & B and hip hop.

🚇 D12 ✉ 1455 rue Crescent ☎ 514/288–0616 🕐 Tue–Fri 5pm–3am, Sat–Sun 9pm–3am 🚇 Guy-Concordia

FAMOUS PLAYERS PARAMOUNT

www.famousplayers.com
Downtown center with 15 theaters—two with IMAX screens—that show films in French and English.

🚇 D12 ✉ 977 rue Sainte-Catherine Ouest
☎ 514/842–5828 🚇 McGill

MCGILL CHAMBER ORCHESTRA

Performs at the Place des Arts and another key classical venue, the Pollack Hall.

🚇 D11 ✉ 555 rue Sherbrooke Ouest
☎ 514/398–4535 🚇 McGill

PLACE DES ARTS

www.pdarts.com
Montréal's showcase for the performing arts has five major performance spaces and houses the Orchestre Symphonique de Montréal, Orchestre Métropolitan de Montréal, Opéra de Montréal and the city's principal ballet troupe, Les Grands Ballets Canadiens. Chamber music, plays, other concerts and an informal Sunday-morning breakfast concert series are also held here.

🚇 E10 ✉ 260 boulevard de Maisonneuve Ouest
☎ Information 514/285–4200, tickets 514/842–2112 🕐 Box office Mon–Fri 10–6 🚇 Place-des-Arts

PUB SIR WINSTON CHURCHILL

English-style pub, known as "Winnies," with a dance floor.

🚇 D12 ✉ 1459 rue Crescent ☎ 514/288–3814 🕐 Daily 11.30am–3am 🚇 Peel, Guy-Concordia

PUB LE VIEUX DUBLIN

A much-loved Irish pub. Live Celtic music nights.

🚇 E12 ✉ 1219a rue University, near rue Sainte-Catherine Ouest
☎ 514/861–4448 🕐 Daily 11am–3am 🚇 McGill

SALSATHÈQUE

Popular downtown Latin club; live music in addition to house DJs.

🚇 D12 ✉ 1220 rue Peel at rue Sainte-Catherine Ouest
☎ 514/875–0016 🕐 Wed–Sat 10pm–3am 🚇 Peel

STOGIE'S CIGAR LOUNGE

www.stogiescigars.ca
In the middle of a fashionable part of Downtown. Anti-smoking proselytism not welcome.

🚇 D12 ✉ 2015 rue Crescent ☎ 514/848–0069 🕐 Daily 11am–3am 🚇 Guy-Concordia

---

THE NAME'S THE GAME

If a friendly local suggests a watering hole make sure you get the full name and the address. Because of the way the French language works and because of the loose definitions Québécois use, a place called, let's say, Au Henri could be listed under Bar Au Henri, Bistro Au Henri, Café Au Henri, Club Au Henri, Restaurant Au Henri, Salon Au Henri, or maybe even Au Henry, which could keep your fingers walking through the phone book for a while.

Restaurants

PRICES

Prices are approximate, based on a 3-course meal for one person.

$$$	over $40
$$	$20–$40
$	under $20

L'ACTUEL ($$)

This noisy downtown café is known for its Belgian dishes, offering variations on the theme of mussels and French fries.
➕ D12 ✉ 1194 rue Peel
☎ 514/866–1537 🕐 Mon–Fri lunch, dinner, Sat dinner only 🚇 Peel, Bonaventure

AMBIANCE ($)

This quirky spot on Antique Row serves salads, sandwiches and imaginatively sauced pastas. Busy at lunch.
➕ E14 ✉ 1874 rue Notre-Dame Ouest
☎ 514/939–2609
🕐 Mon–Fri lunch, Thu and Fri dinner only 🚇 Lucien-l'Allier

AU BISTRO GOURMET ($$)

Classic bistro food: kidney in dijonaise sauce, mussels in pullet sauce.
➕ C13 ✉ 2100 rue Saint-Mathieu ☎ 514/846–1553
🕐 Mon–Fri lunch, dinner, Sat, Sun dinner only

BENS ($)

Opened in 1908 by Ben Kravitz and still run by his grandsons, this garishly lit barn is popular with clubbers and late moviegoers.
➕ D11 ✉ 990 boulevard de Maisonneuve
☎ 514/844–1000 🕐 Daily breakfast, lunch and dinner, until 5am 🚇 Peel

LES CAPRICES DE NICHOLAS ($$$)

The atrium garden of this prettily decorated, three-room restaurant is the perfect place for truffle-scented warm quail and spinach salad.
➕ D12 ✉ 2072 rue Drummond ☎ 514/282–9790
🕐 Daily lunch, dinner
🚇 Peel ❓ Reservations

CAVALLI ($$$)

Sophisticated Italian food with Asian and other overtones seduces a chic and youngish crowd to this smart restaurant. The vivid interior, in pinks, blacks and green, is stylish, and part-open to the street in summer.

OPEN-AIR CAFÉS

Good coffee and reasonably priced snacks are available in just about any open-air café. Find a busy one, pick a sunny table, and sit for as long as you want. The 50 or so cafés in the A. L. Van Houtte chain, are very reliable. Other good locally owned chains are the Brulerie Saint-Denis and the Café Depôt. The Toronto-based Second Cup is making serious inroads, sprouting up all over the place and the US giant Starbuck's, has started to proliferate.

➕ D12 ✉ 2040 rue Peel, near rue Sherbrooke
☎ 514/843–5100 🕐 Mon–Fri lunch, dinner daily 🚇 Peel

LE CAVEAU ($$)

French cooking in a three-story town house. The upper levels are airier.
➕ D11 ✉ 2063 rue Victoria, between rue Sherbooke Ouest and avenue du Président-Kennedy ☎ 514/844–1624
🕐 Mon–Fri lunch, dinner, Sat, Sun dinner only 🚇 McGill
❓ Reservations

CHEZ LA MÈRE MICHEL ($$$)

Perfect dishes—lobster soufflé Mantua, bison and caribou in season—at this well known downtown restaurant.
➕ D13 ✉ 1209 rue Guy
☎ 514/934–0473 🕐 Daily dinner only 🚇 Guy-Concordia ❓ Reservations

ENTRECÔTE SAINT-JEAN ($)

Bistro decor with a simple and inexpensive menu—walnut salad, sirloin, perfect crunchy fries and chocolate profiteroles.
➕ D12 ✉ 2022 rue Peel
☎ 514/281–6492
🕐 Mon–Fri lunch, dinner, Sat, Sun dinner 🚇 Peel

LE LATINI ($$$)

Lavish Italian restaurant with a terrace for alfresco summer dining.
➕ E11 ✉ 1130 rue Jeanne-Mance ☎ 514/861–3166
🕐 Mon–Fri lunch, Sat–Sun dinner only 🚇 Place-d'Armes, Place-des-Arts ❓ Reservations

LE MAS DES OLIVIERS ($$$)

Chef-owner Jacques Muller fills his clients' plates with such deeply satisfying dishes as lamb loin with marrow in port sauce, and quail in puff pastry. And the *pescadou et sa rouquine*, an aromatic fish soup, is superb.
D13 ⊠ 1216 rue Bishop
☎ 514/861–6733
Mon–Fri lunch, dinner, Sat, Sun dinner ⓖ Guy-Concordia
Reservations

MR. STEER ($)

A simple steak-house with leatherette booths serving great burgers.
D12 ⊠ 1198 rue Saint-Catherine Ouest
☎ 514/866–3233 Daily lunch, dinner ⓖ Peel

ORCHIDÉE DE CHINE ($$$)

Best of the Tuxedo Chinese restaurants: flash-fried spinach and dumpling with peanut sauce served in an elegantly simple setting.
D12 ⊠ 2017 rue Peel
☎ 514/287–1878 Mon–Fri lunch, dinner, Sat dinner
ⓖ Peel

LE PARIS ($$)

This downtown restaurant has been serving such comfort dishes as grilled blood pudding, cod brandade and calf's liver neunière since 1956.
D12 ⊠ 1812 rue Sainte-Catherine Ouest
☎ 514/937–4898
Mon–Sat lunch, dinner, Sun dinner ⓖ Guy-Concordia
Reservations

QUEUE DE CHEVAL ($$$)

www.queuedecheval.com
Classy steak-house with prices to match. Well-aged, thick, marbled slabs of beef are sold by weight and seared at an open grill. Conspicuous consumption will result in a tight belt and a thin wallet.
D12 ⊠ 1221 boulevard René-Lévesque Ouest
☎ 514/390–0090 Daily lunch, dinner ⓖ Lucien-L'Allier

LA RAPIERE ($$$)

A stone's throw from Square-Dorchester, this upscale and central restaurant is perfect for an expensive treat, with sublime food based on the regional cuisine of southwest France. Dress up so you won't feel out of place in the elegant dining room.
D12 ⊠ Sun Life Building, 1155 rue Metcalfe
☎ 514/871–8920
Mon–Fri lunch, Mon–Sat dinner ⓖ Peel, Bonaventure

RESTAURANT JULIEN ($$$)

Fashionable downtown restaurant with a canopied terrace to eat outside in summer.
D11 ⊠ 1191 rue Union
☎ 514/871–1581 Mon–Fri lunch, dinner, Sat dinner
ⓖ McGill Reservations

RUBY ROUGE

Very large Chinatown restaurant, popular with Chinese-Canadian and other families, especially at lunch for dim sum. Lotté-Furama is a similar place in the same street at No. 115 (☎ 514/393-3838).
F11 ⊠ 1008 rue Clark
☎ 514/390–8828 Both daily lunch and dinner
ⓖ Place d'Armes

LA TAJ

North Indian specialties, including good tandoori and vegetarian options, at very fair prices.
D12 ⊠ 2077 rue Stanley, near boulevard de Maisonneuve
☎ 514/845–9015
Mon–Sat lunch, dinner daily ⓖ Peel

CHEAP EATS

The best food court in town is upstairs in Le Faubourg Sainte-Catherine (⊠ 1616 rue Sainte-Catherine Ouest). It features a multifarious array of independents selling Moroccan, Italian, Szechuan, Lebanese and Mexican dishes. The food courts in the Gare Centrale, Complexe Desjardins and Place Ville-Marie are a cut above the usual with stalls selling pastries, Mexican food, grilled sausages, smoked meat as well as the usual offerings of chicken, burgers, and fries.

A glorious park protects the heights of Mont-Royal providing fine walks and sweeping views across the city. Between here and Parc La Fontaine are the Quartier Latin and other funky neighborhoods.

Mont-Royal to Parc Lafontaine

PLATEAU
MONT-ROYAL

Palais
des Nains

Ruelle de Mentana

Rue Marie-Anne Est

RACHEL EST

AVENUE

Rue

avenue

St-Christophe

Duluth Est

Châteaubriand

RUE

de

Rivard

RUE DES PINS EST

LAFONTAINE

Rue St-Denis

Théâtre
d'Aujourd'hui

Henri-Julien Est

ST-JEAN
BAPTISTE

Église
St-Jean-Baptiste

RACHEL EST

Rue Marie-Anne Ouest

Rue

Avenue

Avenue

RUE

de

Rue Marie-Anne Ouest

BOULEVARD

RUE

RUE

Duluth

l'Hôtel-de-Ville

Napoléon

Bullion

Roy

Clark

Colonniale

ST-LAURENT

ST-URBAIN

Rue

Bagg

Rue St-Dominique

Rue Coloniale

Rue Guilbault

Rue Sewell

Théâtre
de Quat'
Sous

Théâtre
La Chapelle

Parc

Avenue

de

Jeanne-

Mance

AVENUE

DU

Monument
Sir George-Étienne
Cartier

Musée des
Hospitalières

DES

PINS

OUEST

Rue

Rue

Rue

Hôpital
Thoracique

AVENUE

MILTON PARK

PARC

AVENUE

Arthur

Ste-Famil

La Belvédère
Camillien-Houde

Voie

Camillien-Houde

Centre Int d'Art
Contemporain

Jeanne
Mance

DU

Rue

Rue

Prince

Aylmer

Rue

Rue

Hutchison

PARC

Cimetière de
Notre-Dame-des-Neiges

Croix
234

Institute de
Neurologie

Rue University

PINS

Lorne

Durocher

Aylmer

OUEST

RUE

Hôpital
Royal Victoria

DES

AVENUE

DOCTEUR-PENFIELD

Pollack Hall

Parc du
Mont-Royal

Chemin
Remembrance

Parc
Rutherford

McGill
University

UNIVERSITY

Royal
Victoria
College

AVENUE

Purvis
Hall

RUE

MacTavish

Grand
Châlet

McIntyre
Medical
Sciences

PEEL

Redpath

Circuit

Rue

Rue

DOCTEUR-PENFIELD

138

P

Drummond

Rue

Hôpital
Shriners

ST-ANDRÉ

Avenue Cedar

DES

PINS

OUEST

AVENUE

Rue

de la Montagne

Maison
Alcan

Peel

Peel

Stanley

Avenue du Musée

Rue

Rue

RUE DE LA MONTAGNE

Musée des
Beaux-Arts

SHERBROOKE OUEST

Drummond

Rue Simpson

Redpath

RUE

Crescent

0   250 m

0   250 yds

7

8

9

10

11

12

B   C   D

Parc Lafontaine

Avenue Calixa-Lavallée

Rue

Rue
Hôpital
Notre-Dame

AVENUE PAPINEAU

Théâtre
de Lion d'Or

DU PARC

Université
du Québec
à Montréal

Rue

Rue

Alexandre

Fontaine

Champlain

de

Napoléon

LAFONTAINE

Parc
Persile-
Lachapelle

Sève Dalcourt

de

Est

Rue

Théâtre
Prospero

EST

Rue

TERRASSE ONTARIO

Rue

Rue

de

Logan

Plessis

panet

Mentana

Bouquet

Cherrier

Rue

EST

de

Rue Dalcourt

ST-HUBERT

St-André

Marché
St-Jacques

Beaudry

Rue

La

Rue

Écomusée du
Fier Monde

RUE

Robin

St-Timothée

St-André

The Village

EST

EST

Berri

Studio de
l'Agora
de la Danse

Rue

Rue

ONTARIO

Labrecque

Wolfe

Beaudry

Montcalm

Beaudry

Wolfe

RRSSSMC

Sherbrooke

Rue

Rue

Parc
St-Jacques

MAISONNEUVE

ST-DENIS

SHERBROOKE

St-Christophe

St-Christophe

AMHERST

Rue Sherbrooke

Rue

St-Christophe

STE-CATHERINE

Théâtre
Olympia

Drolet

Square
St-Louis

ST-JACQUES

Rue de la Providence

Rue

ST-HUBERT

Misericordia

Est

ST-LOUIS

RUE

Avenue

Station Centrale
d'Autobus

Parc
Émile-
Gamelin

Rue St-Christophe

Berri

Est

Rue Prince Arthur

Avenue

de

CÉGEP
du Vieux
Montréal

Bibliothèque
Nat

Savoie

Berri-
UQAM

ST-HUBERT

Berri

Labelle

Clark

de

Hôtel-de-Ville

Emery

Université
du Québec
à Montréal
(UQAM)

Cauchetiere

Cinémathèque
Québécoise

Chapelle
Notre-Dame-
de Lourdes

ST-DENIS

Bullion

QUARTIER
LATIN

BOULEVARD

Sanguinet

St-Luc

RENÉ-LÉVESQUE

Musée Juste
Pour Rire

Parc
Hab J.-Mance

Saint-
Laurent

Rue de Boisbriand

Avenue

Rue
Ste-Elisabeth

Rue

Hôtel-de-Ville

Milton

BOULEVARD

RUE

Place
Albert-
Duquesne

ST-LAURENT

Avenue de

St-Dominique

R Berger

Rue

BOULEVARD

Bullion

UQAM
Centre-Design

Rue Kimberley

Place-
des-Artes

ST-URBAIN

Clark

E   F

McGill University

- Roddick Gates
- Green space
- Redpath Museum
- Views
- Arts Building

- Visit the website for details of talks and the museum's winter lecture schedule.
- Special children's workshops are held every Sunday at 1.30 for 4- to 7-year-olds and 3pm for 8- to 12-year-olds.

If you stand on the stone steps of McGill's glass-and-concrete Leacock Building when the snow is falling, and look out across the whitened campus at the glittering city towers, you could fall in love with winter.

Urban country The university opened in 1821 on Mont-Royal's lower slopes on a patch of pasture donated for the purpose by fur trader and land speculator James McGill. Since then, Montréal has spread northwards and now surrounds the 32ha (80-acre) campus. McGill offers a privileged place from which to view the city and feel its vibrant rhythms.

Architecture The Greek Revival Roddick Gates guard the main entrance to the university on rue

New halls of residence (left) at McGill University, where life as a student is a memorable experience
University Street, exciting and vibrant at night (right)

Sherbrooke Ouest, and behind them a tree-lined avenue leads to the 1839 neoclassical domed Arts Building, the oldest of the 70 or so buildings on campus. Inside is Moyse Hall, a lovely theater dating from 1926. Along the avenue's east side are two fine neoclassical buildings designed by Sir Andrew Taylor in the 1890s, who also designed the Library with its elaborately carved columns and gargoyles. Percy Nobbs's 1908 Macdonald Engineering Building is a remarkable example of the English Baroque Revival style. But the most beautiful structure on campus is the templelike Redpath Museum of Natural History, refurbished in 2001 and one of Canada's oldest museums; it houses a huge and wonderfully whimsical collection that includes dinosaur bones, old coins, African art and a shrunken head. Under the trees a bronze James McGill hurries across campus.

THE BASICS

www.mcgill.ca/redpath

✚ D11

✉ 859 rue Sherbrooke Ouest

☎ Redpath Museum 514/398–4086

🕐 Labor Day–late Jun Mon–Fri 9–5, Sun 1–5. Late Jun–Labor Day Mon–Thu 9–5, Sun 1–5

🚇 McGill

♿ Fair

💲 Free

Parc du Mont-Royal

HIGHLIGHTS

● Montréal Cross
● Le Chalet viewpoint
● Beaver Lake
● Cimetière Notre-Dame-des-Neiges
● Mont-Royal Cemetery

TIPS

● The visitor center, Smith House, is midway between Beaver Lake and Le Chalet at 1260 Remembrance Road.
● Café Smith offers drinks, snacks and light meals and has an outdoor terrace.

Mont-Royal is only 233m (764ft) above sea level but Montréalers call it, without irony, "the Mountain," an appropriately grand appellation given the hold this steep, green oasis has on their affection.

Park on the hill Mont-Royal is one of seven such peaks on the St. Lawrence plain, all composed of intrusive rock hard enough to have survived the glacial erosion of the last Ice Age. Explorer Jacques Cartier named the hill—probably in honor of his royal patron, Francis I of France—on his first voyage up the St. Lawrence in 1535. The area became a park in 1877, following the local council's fear that the forested slopes were being denuded by Montréalers' quest for firewood. The land was bought for $1 million, and landscaped by designer Frederick Law Olmsted, also responsible for New

*Apart from the many activities to take part in at Parc du Mont-Royal, there are spectac-
ular views of the city, at best in the early evening when the city lights up*

York's Central Park and San Francisco's Golden
Gate Park.

So much to do The park is too large to see in a
day, so pick a corner to explore. Most people on
foot enter at the Monument Sir George-Étienne
Cartier, a popular summer venue for street musicians, vendors and people-watchers. Olmsted
Road leads to the Montréal Cross (1924) on the
summit. Beaver Lake, created in the 1930s, is
another focal point, as is Le Chalet, which has fan-
tastic views and is close to a visitor center. Calixa
Lavallée, composer of Canada's national anthem,
is buried in the Roman Catholic Cimetière Notre-
Dame-des-Neiges, one of two cemeteries on the
northern perimeter, and Ann Leonowens, immor-
talized in *The King and I*, is interred in the
Protestant Mont-Royal Cemetery.

THE BASICS

www.lemontroyal.qc.ca
🞧 B11
✉ Monument Sir George-
Étienne Cartier and other
entrances
☎ 514/843–8240
🕐 Daily 6am–midnight
🍴 The Chalet
🚇 Mont-Royal
🚌 11, 66, 80, 107, 129,
144, 165
♿ Some steep paths
👆 Free

Musée des Beaux-Arts

A painting Mah-Min (1848) by Paul Kane (left) displayed in the museum (below)

THE BASICS

www.mmfa.qc.ca

🔼 C12

✉ 1379–1384 rue Sherbrooke Ouest

☎ 514/285–2000

🕐 Tue, Wed, Thu–Sun 11–5

🍴 Café des Beaux-Arts; also cafeteria

🚇 Guy-Concordia

🚌 24

♿ Good

📋 Free permanent exhibition. Special shows expensive

HIGHLIGHTS

● *Portrait of a Young Woman*, Rembrandt
● *Portrait of a Man*, El Greco
● *Torso*, Henry Moore
● *October*, James Tissot

Canada's oldest art museum (founded in 1860) consists of the Museum of Fine Arts and its magnificent and more recent Desmarais Pavilion, and has the best collection of Canadian paintings in the country, as well as First Nations artifacts, and many fine old masters.

A fine museum This venerable institution is one of North America's finest galleries. Completed in 1912 and enlarged in 1976, the main building is unmistakable, with its stolid Vermont marble front and four large Ionic columns. Across the street stands the Desmarais Pavilion (1991), a stunning modern building designed by Montréal architect Moshe Safdie. Wonderful views across the city open up from its upper levels, and underground galleries connect it with the original building.

The collection Canadian paintings range from works imported by the early French settlers through to those by artists from the Toronto-based Group of Seven. Look for the fine landscapes, and paintings by the so-called Automatistes, who dominated Montréal's art world during the 1940s. First Nations objects are on display, along with period furnishings, drawings, engravings, silverware and art from ancient China, Japan, Egypt, Greece and South America. Among the old masters are works by Rembrandt, El Greco and Memlinc; Picasso, Henry Moore and Impressionists represent more recent eras. The museum has absorbed the defunct Musée des Arts Décoratifs and displays its collection of ceramics, fabrics and furniture.

More to See

CHAPELLE NOTRE-DAME-DE-LOURDES

The Quartier Latin's Our Lady of Lourdes Chapel faces the old church of Saint-Jacques, hidden behind a bland exterior. But its sumptuously decorated interior, a mixture of Romanesque and Byzantine styles that dates from 1876, has vivid murals—the work of artist Napoléon Bourassa.

➕ F9 ✉ 430 rue-Sainte-Catherine Est ☎ 514/842–4704 ⏰ Mon–Sat 7.30–6 or later, Sun 9–6 Ⓜ Berri-UQAM

ÉCOMUSÉE DU FIER MONDE

www.ecomusee.qc.ca

Photographs and period objects are used to illustrate the Industrial Revolution and its impact on Montréal and its people.

➕ E8 ✉ 2050 rue Amherst ☎ 514/528–8444 ⏰ Wed 11–8, Thu–Fri 9.30–4, Sat–Sun 10.30–5 Ⓜ Sherbrooke, Berri-UQAM 🚌 24 ♿ Good 💰 Moderate

MAISON ALCAN

The Aluminum Company of Canada headquarters designed by Montréal architect Rag Affleck (1983) blends old and new, and it has a stunning atrium.

➕ D12 ✉ 1188 rue Sherbrooke Ouest ☎ 514/848–8000 ♿ Very good Ⓜ Peel ❓ Guided tours. Free lunchtime concerts

MUSÉE DES HOSPITALIÈRES

www.museedeshospitalieres.qc.ca

The museum tells the story of the Hôtel-Dieu, Montréal's first hospital, and the Hospitalières de Saint-Joseph, recruited in France in 1659 by Montréal's co-founder, Jeanne Mance.

➕ D10 ✉ 201 avenue des Pins Ouest ☎ 514/849–2919 ⏰ Mid-Jun to mid-Oct Tue–Fri 10–5, Sat, Sun 1–5; mid-Oct to mid-Jun Wed–Sun 1–5 Ⓜ Sherbrooke 🚌 144 ♿ Fair 💰 Inexpensive

MUSÉE JUSTE POUR RIRE

Film clips, stage sets, cartoons and costumes are used to trace the history of comedy.

➕ E10 ✉ 2111 boulevard Saint-Laurent ☎ 514/845–5105 ⏰ Hours vary; call to confirm times 🍴 Café Ⓜ Saint-Laurent 🚌 24, 55 💰 Inexpensive

Écomusée du Fier Monde

PARC LAFONTAINE

Lafontaine divides into an English-style landscape in the west and a French-style garden in the east, with tennis courts, outdoor swimming pools and summer concerts.

➕ E7 ✉ Rue Sherbrooke Est, between rue Saint-Hubert and avenue Papineau 🕐 Daily 9am–10pm 🍴 Snack bar 🚇 Sherbrooke (8-block walk) ♿ Good ⌨ Free

RUE SAINT-DENIS

Rue Saint-Denis bisects Montréal's Quartier Latin, a slightly seedy area that is now being filled with interesting cafés, bistros and shops.

➕ D8 🚇 Berri-UQAM, Sherbrooke

RUE SHERBROOKE

The most interesting section of this street flanks an area whose residents were once estimated to own 70 per-cent of Canada's wealth. You can still find luxury shops, hotels and galleries.

➕ E9 🚇 Peel, McGill

SQUARE SAINT-LOUIS

This leafy square was laid out in 1879, away from downtown and the Vieux-Port, and is considered one of the city's finest. Its beautiful houses are now home to poets, artists and writers attracted by the Bohemian atmos-phere of the surrounding Saint-Denis district. At its southern end lies the pedestrians-only rue Prince-Arthur Est, full of street entertainers in summer.

➕ E9 🚇 Sherbrooke

THE VILLAGE

The Village is the name given to an area that forms the heart of Montréal's vibrant and blossoming gay and les-bian community. A few blocks from the Quartier Latin, it is on rue Sainte-Catherine between rue Amhurst and rue Papineau. Gay or straight, anyone will enjoy exploring the more than 100 design shops, bars, clubs, cafés and small restaurants that serve the community, which has transformed a formerly rundown area of the city. The area is especially lively during the 800,000-strong gay and lesbian parade in July.

➕ F8 🚇 Beaudry or Papineau

Relaxing in the sun at Parc Lafontaine

Parks and Views

A walk that offers a taste of Montréal's loveliest park and provides a majestic overview of the city from its various panoramic lookouts.

DISTANCE: (5–7km) 3–4 miles   **ALLOW:** 2–3 hours

START

MONUMENT SIR GEORGE-ETIENNE CARTIER ✚ C9 🚇 Mont-Royal

END

RUE DES PINS OUEST ✚ C11 🚇 Peel

❶ Take a cab to the Monument Sir George-Étienne Cartier, a popular spot and the main northern entrance to Parc du Mont-Royal (▷ 72).

❽ From here you can walk to sights such as the McCord Museum (▷ 52), McGill University (▷ 70) or Musée des Beaux-Arts (▷ 74).

❷ Follow the looping chemin Olmsted up through the park, a 4.8km (3-mile) gravel path created by the park's designer to accommodate horse-drawn carriages.

❼ At the end of the chemin Olmsted, the rustic Chalet offers another café and superb views over the city. Retrace your steps, or take the steps, and follow Redpath Crescent to rue des Pins Ouest.

❸ At several points in the park you can see the Croix sur la Montage, a landmark erected in 1924 and visible across the city. Impressive from afar, so do not be tempted from the paths.

❻ Above the lake, walk through the sculpture garden to the Maison Smith, which has a visitor center and café.

❹ About midway up the chemin Olmsted, 200 steps provide a short-cut to Le Chalet du Mont-Royal. Take this if you are fit, but otherwise continue on the chemin Olmsted.

❺ The path curves round to a grassy area around Lac-des-Castors (Beaver Lake), a popular place for summer and winter activities.

Shopping

AIME COM MOI

A great boutique for the latest in exclusive high-quality fashions for women, mostly from Montréal and Québec-based designers.

✚ C8 ✉ 150 avenue du Mont-Royal Est
☎ 514/982–0088
🕐 Mon–Wed 12–6, Thu–Fri 12–9, Sat 11–5, Sun 12–5
🚇 Mont-Royal

ARCHAMBAULT

www.archambault.ca
Montréal's own music shop is excellent for current releases, classical music and Québec pop. It also has an extensive selection of song books and sheet music.

✚ E10 ✉ 175 rue Sainte-Catherine Est ☎ 514 849–6201 🕐 Mon–Wed 9.30–6, Thu, Fri 9.30–9, Sat, Sun 11–5 🚇 Berri-UQAM

BELLA PELLA

www.bellapella.com
Bella Pella is Italian for "Beautiful Skin," and this scented shops sells lotions, potions, soaps, shampoos and other body-care products, most of them made with organic products by small, local producers.

✚ D9 ✉ 3933 rue Saint-Denis ☎ 514/845–7328
🕐 Mon–Wed 11–6, Thu–Fri 11–9, Sat 11–5, Sun 12–5
🚇 Mont-Royal

CHAPOFOLIE

Both men and women can complete their fashion purchases here, at the largest hat store in the city.

✚ D9 ✉ 3944 rue Saint-Denis ☎ 514/982–0036
🕐 Mon–Thu 11–6, Fri 11–9, Sat 11–5, Sun 1–5 🚇 Mont-Royal

LES COURS MONT-ROYAL

This elegant shopping center is in the old Mount Royal Hotel, a jazz-age palace that was the largest hotel in the British Empire when it opened in 1922. When developers gutted the place in 1987, they left the exterior intact and saved part of the old lobby with a crystal chandelier that used to illuminate the Monte Carlo Casino. The inner court rises 10 stories to the roof, and is surrounded by balconies and fashionable shops.

✚ D12 ✉ 1550 rue Metcalfe ☎ 514/842–7777 🚇 Peel

FURS

Montréal owes its early commercial success to the fur trades, and trends away from the wearing of furs notwithstanding, the city still boasts some of Canada's best furriers. Grosvenor-McComber (✉ 402 boulevard de Maisonneuve Ouest ☎ 514/288–1255) has been in business since 1895. Birger Christensen at Holt Renfrew (✉ 1300 rue Sherbrooke Ouest ☎ 514/842–5111) is a favorite among the city elite.

DUBUC MODE DE VIE

www.dubecstyle.com
Philippe Dubuc is one of the premier designers of both men's and women's clothes in Canada. This stylish boutique in the Plateau Mont-Royal district is his headquarters and displays both collections in gorgeous surroundings.

✚ D9 ✉ 4451 rue Saint-Denis ☎ 514/282–1424
🕐 Mon–Wed 10.30–6 Thu, Fri 10.30–9, Sat 10.30–5, Sun 1–5
🚇 Mont-Royal

LE FAUBOURG SAINTE-CATHERINE

The Faubourg complex is easily accessible from downtown. Clothing and craft outlets compete with food, fruit and vegetable stalls over three levels while inexpensive cafés and food kiosks surround a central atrium.

✚ D13 ✉ Rue Guy at 1616 rue Sainte-Catherine Ouest ☎ 514/939–3663 🕐 Daily 9am–9.30pm 🚇 Guy-Concordia

GIORGIO

Two chic stores offer top names in men's and women's high fashion.

✚ D12 ✉ Giorgio Femme (women): Le Cours Mont-Royal, 1455 rue Peel ☎ 514/282–0294 ✉ Giorgio Montréal (men): Maison Alcan, 1176 rue Sherbrooke Ouest ☎ 514/287–1928
🕐 Mon–Wed 9.30–6, Thu, Fri 9.30–9, Sat 9.30–6 🚇 Peel

GUILDE CANADIENNE DES MÉTIERS D'ART

www.canadianguild.com

Canadian crafts such as blown glass, porcelain, pewter, tapestry and jewlry, plus a permanent exhibition of Inuit, First Peoples and other Canadian sculpture, prints and artifacts.
🏠 C12 ✉ 1460 rue Sherbrooke Ouest
☎ 514/849–6091 🕐 Tue–Fri 10–6, Sat 10–5 🚇 Guy-Concordia

HMV
www.hmv.com
Airy, comprehensive and well organized—the best place to buy CDs and audiocassettes.
🏠 D12 ✉ 1020 rue Sainte-Catherine Ouest
☎ 514/875–0765
🕐 Mon–Fri 9–9, Sat 9–5, Sun 10–5 🚇 Peel

HOLT RENFREW
www.holtrenfrew.com
Established in 1837, this is the oldest of the city's large stores, and has occupied its present distinctive six-story home since 1936. It is particularly known for its furs, and has supplied four generations of British royalty (among others), but also sells other quality goods and fashions.
🏠 C12 ✉ 300 rue Sherbrooke Ouest at rue de la Montagne ☎ 514/842–5111
🕐 Mon–Wed 10–6, Thu, Fri 10–9, Sat 10–6, Sun 11.30
🚇 Peel

KANUK
www.kanuk.com
Here you can uncover everything you need to survive when the temperature drops. The coats, sleeping bags and items are widely available, but you'll find the keenest prices here at the factory store.
🏠 D8 ✉ 485 rue Rachel Est
☎ 514/284–4494 or 877/284–4494 🕐 Mon–Wed 9–6, Thu, Fri 9–9, Sat 10–5, Sun 12–5 🚇 Mont-Royal
🚌 30

NADYA TOTO
Nadya Toto designs modern, elegantly casual but reasonably priced clothes for women 25 to 55. This young designer often works with a wool-Spandex mix that gives her clothes comfort and softness.
🏠 D12 ✉ 2057 rue de la Montagne ☎ 514/350–9090
🕐 Mon–Wed 10–5, Thu, Fri 11–7, Sat 11–5, Sun 12–5
🚇 Peel

WHERE TO LOOK
Antiques hunters with thick wallets search for treasures in the lavish shops along rue Sherbrooke Ouest and in exclusive Westmount. The more modest crowd look on trendy Antique Alley on rue Notre-Dame Ouest. Real hunters haunt the shops on rue Amherst, where they can buy wooden toys in Antiquités Curiosités at No. 1769, or scavenge chrome fittings from the 1950s in Cité Déco at No. 1761.

OGILVY
www.ogilvycanada.com
A favorite among affluent Montréalers, Ogilvy has been in business since 1866. The emphasis here is on luxury goods, mainly items of clothing.
🏠 D12 ✉ 1307 rue Sainte-Catherine Ouest at rue de la Montagne ☎ 514/842–7711
🕐 Mon–Wed 10–6, Thu, Fri 10–9, Sat 9–5, Sun 12–5
🚇 Peel

SCARLETT O'HARA
www.boutiquescarlett.com
Ultra-trendy shop with its own line of daring women's fashions.
🏠 C8 ✉ 254 avenue Mont-Royal Est ☎ 514/844–9435
🕐 Mon–Wed 11–6, Thu, Fri 11–9, Sat 11–5, Sun 12–5
🚇 Mont-Royal

UNIVERSITÉ MCGILL
Well-stocked and intelligent book shelves.
🏠 D11 ✉ 420 rue McTavish
☎ 514/398–7444
🕐 Mon–Sat 8.30am–10pm
🚇 Peel

VALE D'COEUR
www.valet.com
This is a shop for children and adults of all ages, and sells an excellent range of board games, comics, posters and toys. Its range of chess sets and boards is second to none.
🏠 C8 ✉ 4408 rue Saint-Denis ☎ 514/499–9970
🕐 Mon–Wed 11.30–6, Thu–Fri 11.30–9, Sat 10–5, Sun 11.30–5
🚇 Mont-Royal

Entertainment and Nightlife

LE BALATTOU
www.festivalnuitsdafrique.com
A welcoming (if hot and crowded) dance club with an African and tropical motif.
➕ C8 ✉ 4372 boulevard Saint-Laurent ☎ 514/845–5447 🕐 Tue–Sun 9pm–3am
🚇 29, 55

BALLROOM
Loft-style space with a bar, DJs and dancing.
➕ D9 ✉ 3643 boulevard Saint-Laurent
☎ 514/282–POOL
🕐 Wed–Sun 9pm–3am
🚇 Saint-Laurent

BELMONT
Quiet bar with plenty of room to sit and talk. A disco is to the rear. Lines on weekends.
➕ C8 ✉ 4483 boulevard Saint-Laurent ☎ 514/845–8443 🕐 Thu–Sat 8pm–3am
🚇 29, 55 ✋ Cover charge on weekends

BISTRO A JOJO
www.bistroajojo.com
A relaxed and intimate blues club that's been in business since 1975. Come early to be sure of one of the simple wooden chairs at the close-packed tables.
➕ E9 ✉ 1627 rue St-Denis
☎ 514/843–5015 🕐 Shows nightly from 10pm 🚇 Berri-UQAM

CAFÉ CENTRAL
Small, relaxed and convenient to shopping. Occasional live music.
➕ C8 ✉ 4479 rue Saint-Denis ☎ 514/845–9010
🕐 Tue–Sun 9pm–3am
🚇 Sherbrooke

LE CHEVAL BLANC
Unchanged for half a century, music combines with the buzz of arty and political talk. Communal tables; beer brewed on-site.
➕ E9 ✉ 809 rue Ontario Est
☎ 514/522–0211 🕐 Daily 3pm–3am 🚇 Berri-UQAM

LE CLUB SODA
www.clubsoda.ca
This is an excellent venue where you can be sure to find good live music (including big international names) and other shows such as comedy.
➕ E10 ✉ 1225 boulevard Saint-Laurent
☎ 514/286–1010 🕐 Daily 8pm–2am 🚇 Saint-Laurent

LES FOUFOUNES ELECTIQUES
www.foufounes.qc.ca
A fixutre of Montréal's

WHERE TO GO?
Clubs and discos are notorious for fading in and out of fashion, or for closing down altogether, so for the latest on clubs check the free magazines to be found at tourist offices, record shops and cafés. *The Mirror*, the *Hour* and the *French Voir* (all free) contain extensive listings of clubs and live music venues, as does *The Montréal Gazette*, the city's main English-language newspaper.

nightlife scene, this club features loud mainstream bands and has three dance floors and a large beer terrace.
➕ E10 ✉ 87 rue Sainte-Catherine Est ☎ 514/844–5539 🚇 Berri-UQAM

JELLO
A 1960s style lounge-club with 50 martinis on offer. Live music nearly every night. Pool tables.
➕ E9 ✉ 151 rue Ontario Est
☎ 514/285–2621 🕐 Tue–Fri 5pm–3am, Sat 9pm–3am
🚇 Saint-Laurent

LE PASSEPORT
By day a curiosity shop, by night a long-running club with good music.
➕ D8 ✉ 4156 rue Saint-Denis ☎ 514/842–6063
🕐 Wed, Fri, Sat from 10pm
🚇 Sherbrooke

QUAI DES BRUMES
Two quite different jazz bars share a building on rue Saint-Denis. Downstairs is the intimate Quai des Brumes. Upstairs is the bigger and louder Café Central, which draws a college crowd.
➕ C8 ✉ 4479 rue Saint-Denis ☎ 514/845–9010
🕐 Daily 2pm–3am 🚇 Mont-Royal

LE SAINT-SULPICE
www.lesaint-sulpice.com
Fashionable Quartier Latin bar, with terraces.
➕ E9 ✉ 1680 rue Saint-Denis, near rue Emery
☎ 514/844–9458 🕐 Daily 12am–3am 🚇 Berri-UQAM

Restaurants

PRICES

Prices are approximate, based on a 3-course meal for one person.

$$$	over $40
$$	$20–$40
$	under $20

À LA DÉCOUVERTE ($$)

Classic French cuisine on a quiet street in the Plateau Mont-Royal. Reserve two weeks in advance for weekends. BYOB.

➕ C7 ✉ 4350 rue de la Roche ☎ 514/529–8377 🕐 Wed–Sat dinner 🚇 Mont-Royal ❓ Reservations essential

AU PIED DE COCHON ($$)

A couple of blocks off rue Saint-Denis, the "Pig's Foot" offers robust and no-nonsense dishes guaranteed to warm on a chill day, with fish and lighter dishes in summer.

➕ D8 ✉ 536 avenue Duluth ☎ 514/281–1114 🕐 Dinner daily 🚇 Sherbrooke, Mont-Royal

BON BLÉ RIZ ($$)

Lamb in a peppery anise-flavored sauce and spicy shrimp are among the flamboyant dishes at this unpretentious restaurant.

➕ E10 ✉ 1437 boulevard Saint-Laurent ☎ 514/844–1447 🕐 Mon–Fri lunch, dinner, Sat dinner 🚇 Saint-Laurent

LA BRIOCHE LYONNAISE ($)

The best pâtisserie in a city known for its cakes and confectioners. The chocolates are out of this world.

➕ E9 ✉ 1593 rue Saint-Denis, between boulevard de Maisonnneuve and rue Emery ☎ 514/842–7017 🕐 Daily breakfast, lunch, dinner 🚇 Berri-UQAM

CAFÉ FERRARI ($$$)

Haute cuisine Portuguese style. Nibble on salted cod and olives while you consider the grilled octopus or the sausages marinated in red wine.

➕ D12 ✉ 1446 rue Peel ☎ 514/848–0988 🕐 Mon–Fri lunch, dinner, Sat dinner 🚇 Peel ❓ Reservations essential

CAFÉ SANTROPOL ($)

www.santropol.com

A charming student café with mainly vegetarian food, and more than 60

POPULAR MESS

Québec's own contribution to fast-food culture is something called *poutine* (literally "mess"). It consists of a huge plate of French fries, covered liberally with lumps of pale yellow cheeze curds and drowned in a gelatinous mass of thick, brown gravy. Another fast-food favorite is barbecued chicken, a crispy skin, spit-roasted bird served with a spicy sauce.

herbal teas on offer. Many ice creams, malts and sodas, and plenty of fruit juices, salads and quiches.

➕ C9 ✉ 3990 rue Saint-Urbain ☎ 514/842–3110 🕐 Daily lunch, dinner 🚇 Sherbrooke

CHU CHAI ($$)

www.chuchai.com

This vegetarian paradise whips up fine renditions of Thai classic dishes with substituted soy or *seitan* for chicken and shrimp.

➕ D8 ✉ 4088 rue Saint-Denis ☎ 514/843–4194 🕐 Daily lunch, dinner 🚇 Sherbrooke, Mont-Royal

L'EXPRESS ($$)

Elbow-to-elbow tables, cheerfully frantic service, perfect food and interesting wines.

➕ D8 ✉ 3927 rue Saint-Denis at rue Duluth ☎ 514/845–5333 🕐 Daily lunch, dinner 🚇 Sherbrooke ❓ Reservations essential

LES GÂTERIES CAFÉ ($)

Haunt of writers and artists. The house coffee is a rich blend of 40 kinds of beans.

➕ E9 ✉ 3443 rue Saint-Denis ☎ 514/843–6235 🕐 Daily breakfast, lunch, dinner 🚇 Sherbrooke

GLOBE ($$$)

www.restaurantglobe.com

The wood, leather and mirror interior is traditional, but the high-quality and well-sourced food at

this popular and fashionable restaurant has a modern slant.

🚩 D9 ⊠ 3455 boulevard Saint-Laurent ☎ 514/284–3823 🕔 Dinner daily 🚇 Saint-Laurent

LE JARDIN DE PANOS ($$)

www.lejardindepanos.com
This is the best of the Greek eateries in the rue Duluth area, with good versions of standard dishes such as calamari and moussaka.

🚩 D8 ⊠ 521 rue Duluth Est ☎ 514/521–4206 🕔 Daily lunch, dinner 🚇 Sherbrooke, Mont-Royal

LA LOUX ($$)

www.laloux.com
Classic French food with a modern edge in a discreet, elegant setting.

🚩 D9 ⊠ 250 avenue des Pins Est ☎ 514/287–9127 🕔 Mon–Fri lunch, dinner, Sat, Sun dinner 🚇 Sherbooke ❓ Reservations

MOISHE'S ($)

www.moishes.ca
Eat marbled steak aged the same way since 1938. A premier steak house, owned and run by the same family since it was opened. Crowded and noisy.

🚩 C9 ⊠ 3961 boulevard Sain-Laurent at rue Duluth ☎ 514/845–3509 🕔 Daily dinner 🚇 Mont-Royal

LA PARYSE ($)

The burgers at this Quartier-Latin spot are

huge. Toppings for designer hamburgers include blue cheese, cream cheese, porcino mushrooms and fresh-grated Parmesan. Very popular with students at the nearby junior college.

🚩 E9 ⊠ 302 rue Ontario Est ☎ 514/842–2040 🕔 Tue–Sun lunch, dinner 🚇 Berri-UQAM

PÂTISSERIE BELGE ($)

This cheerful café/tea-room and shop is an ideal place to stop after a stroll for a *café au lait* and a Belgian chocolate confection. The soup, salads and pâtés are all good.

🚩 D10 ⊠ 3485 avenue du Parc ☎ 514/845–1245 🕔 Restaurant: lunch, early dinner Mon–Sat. Shop: daily Mon–Wed 6pm, Thu–Fri 8pm, Sat 5.30pm, Sun 4.30pm 🚇 Place-des-Arts (then a 10-minute walk)

BRING YOUR OWN BOTTLE

If you're watching your budget, consider dining at a restaurant that allows you to bring your own wine. Entries are designated as "BYOB"– bring your own bottle (*Apporter son vin*). BYOB restaurants are common in Montréal, thanks to a quirk in Québec's provincial liquor laws. The food quality in these places ranges from pedestrian to excellent, but is usually inexpensive.

PHAYA THAI ($)

This good Thai restaurant is typical of the ever-increasing range of ethnic cuisines available in Montréal.

🚩 B8 ⊠ 107 avenue Laurier Ouest ☎ 514/272–3456 🚇 Laurier

PSAROTAVERNA DU SYMPOSIUM ($$)

Fish nets and marine colors set the scene for grilled fresh fish, shrimp and octopus.

🚩 D8 ⊠ 3829 rue Saint-Denis ☎ 514/842–0867 🕔 Mon–Fri lunch, dinner, Sat dinner 🚇 Sherbrooke

SCHWARATZ'S ($)

The three best things on the menu are smoked meat, smoked meat and smoked meat—but the steaks are pretty good too. Famous and packed, expect brusque service and lines.

🚩 D9 ⊠ 3895 boulevard Saint-Laurent at rue Napoléon ☎ 514/842–4813 🕔 Daily lunch, dinner 🚇 Mont-Royal

SAINT-VIATEUR BAGEL & CAFÉ ($)

Bagels at this Montréal classic two blocks east of the Mont-Royal metro are a great way to start the day and also make a good snack before or after a stroll in the nearby Parc Lafontaine.

🚩 C7 ⊠ 1127 avenue Mont-Royal Est ☎ 514/528–6361 🚇 Mont-Royal

The striking stadium and buildings created for the 1976 Olympic Games, along with the Jardin Botanique, one of the world's largest botanical gardens, provide a fine counterpart to Montréal's other attractions.

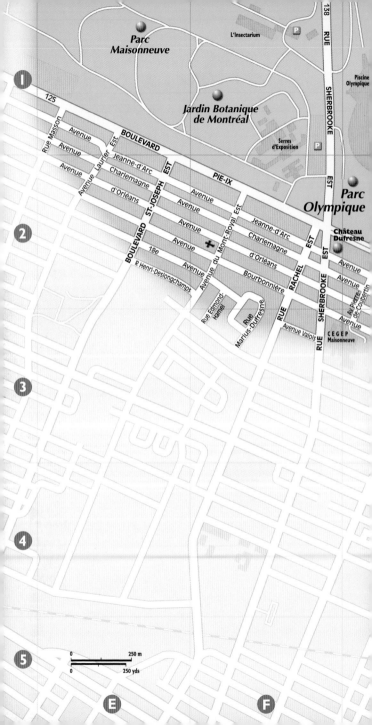

Aréna Maurice-Richard

Centre Pierre-Charbonneau

Viau

Parc Theodore

Rue de Ville-Marie

BOULEVARD

RUE

VIAU

Pierre-de-Coubertin

Biodôme de Montréal

Rue

ST-CLEMENT

Théodore

Rouen

Avenue

HOCHELAGA

Rue

Leclaire

Stade Olympique

Avenue

Rue

Sicard

Aird

MAISONNEUVE

Avenue

P

Bennett

Avenue

de

Parc Ovila Pelletier

Avenue

RUE

Marché Maisonneuve

EST

Pie-IX

Avenue

Létourneux

ONTARIO

BOULEVARD

de

RUE

Charlemagne

Desjardins

Rue

LaSalle

HOCHELAGA

PIE-IX

Avenue

Jeanne-d'Arc

Bourbonnière

RUE

Transformateur

d'Orléans

G

H

Parc Olympique and the North

The Montréal Tower (left), standing guard over the Olympic Stadium (right)

Parc Olympique

During the summer 1976 Olympic Games, the perfect performances of Romanian gymnast Nadia Comanecia thrilled the world. But once over, the games left an architectural and financial legacy that still divides the city.

Soaring costs When Mayor Jean Drapeau persuaded Montréalers to host the Olympic Games in 1976 he promised that the event wouldn't cost them a cent. French architect Roger Taillibert set to work believing money was no object. Both were wrong. The stadium and its tower cost $1.2 (US) billion, and Québec smokers are still paying off the debt with a special tax on tobacco. The stadium itself has never been much of a success as a sports venue, abandoned by the local football team, and the Expos, Montréal's major-league baseball team, regularly threaten to leave. The place makes its money on trade shows and huge concerts. But it's impressively bright and airy, and worth seeing.

Leaning tower It is not so much the stadium that pulls in visitors, it's the park's famous inclined tower (Tour de Montréal), built to support the stadium's retractable roof. Since it opened in 1989, more than 5 million people have ascended to the observation platform. The 175m (575ft) ascent via an external cable car is stomach churning, but you are rewarded with a view that on a clear day stretches for 80km (50 miles). Galleries in the tower's lower levels contain displays about the park's history, and the Tourist Hall at the tower's base has information, tickets and exhibits.

THE BASICS

www.rio.gouv.qc.ca

+ G2

✉ 4141 avenue Pierre-de-Coubertin

☎ 514/252–4141

🕐 Daily late Jun–early Sep 9–7; rest of year daily 9–5. Regular guided tours (call 514/252–4737 or 1-877/997–0919 for latest times)

🍴 Cafés

Ⓥ Viau

🚌 185

♿ Very good

🎟 Tower: expensive. Tours: moderate

❓ Souvenir shop

TIPS

● A free shuttle bus links Viau Métro station to the Parc Olympique, Biodôme and Jardin Botanique–half-hourly from 11–5.

● Regular 30-minute guided tours ($8 adult, $6.25 child) leave regularly from the base of the Tour de Montréal from 10am May–end Aug and 11pm Sep–end Apr.

Biodôme de Montréal

HIGHLIGHTS

● The sloths in the rain forest
● The beaver dam and lodge in the St. Lawrence habitat
● Puffins and penguins in the polar zone

TIPS

● Use the free shuttle bus to travel between the Biodôme, Parc Olympique, Viau Métro, Insectarium and Jardin Botanique.
● Save money; buy joint tickets to the Insectarium and Jardin Botanique.

The Biôdome has been a success ever since it opened in 1992 in what used to be the Olympic velodrome. This living museum integrates birds, animals and plants into superb re-creations of their natural habitats.

Habitats Montréal's Biodôme, the only one of its kind in the world, replicates four of the most beautiful habitats in North, Central and South America—tropical forest, the St. Lawrence marine ecosystem, Laurentian forest, and the polar world—with their plants, birds, marine creatures and other animals. You watch otters frolicking in waterfalls, observe marine creatures through glass and peek at animals and preening birds through the foliage of living forest. But this is more than an indoor zoo. It is actively involved in breeding

Montréal's Biôdome (top left) houses an environmental museum comprising four ecosystems: polar world (top middle, bottom left), St. Lawrence marine (bottom middle), Amazonian rainforest (bottom right) and Laurentian forest
The huge globe provides a central point to touch base (right)

endangered species in captivity with the hope of releasing the offspring into the wild.

Animals As you walk into the first habitat, the Amazonian rain forest, heat, humidity and animal smells hit you like a wall. Exotic birds chirp overhead, while the leafy undergrowth is alive with crocodiles, capybaras and golden lion tamarins (orange-furred monkeys that are increasingly scarce in their native Brazil). You'll also see darting parrots, a cave full of bats (behind glass) and other mammals, amphibians, reptiles and fish. In the Laurentian forest you can watch lynx, otter, beaver and porcupine. A tank in the St. Lawrence marine ecosystem re-creates a sea complete with nesting gannets and a tidal pool filled with sea urchins and anemones. The popular puffins and penguins are in the polar area.

THE BASICS

www.ville.montreal.qc.ca /biodome or
www.biodome.qc.ca
✚ G1
✉ 4777 avenue Pierre-de-Coubertin
☎ 514/868-3000
🕐 Late Jun to early Sep daily 9–6. Early Sep to late-Jun Tue–Sun 9–5; also 9–8.30 during school hols
🍴 Café
🚇 Viau
♿ Very good
💰 Expensive. Combined tickets available (▷ Tips, 88)
❓ Gift shop

Jardin Botanique de Montréal

TOP 25

HIGHLIGHTS

- Summer butterflies
- *Croque Insectes* (insect tastings, which chefs prepare using edible insects)
- Orchids and begonias
- First Nations garden
- The Rose Garden

TIPS

- Check ahead for times of the tea ceremonies in the Japanese Garden Pavilion and the *Croque Insectes*.
- Leave time for the Arboretum, it covers a big area.

Montréal has the world's second-largest botanical gardens—no small feat given the cruel climate. The preserve is a blend of exotic horticulture with the beauty and tranquility of a formal garden.

Gardens Montréal's lovely botanical gardens are the second largest in the world after Kew Gardens in London. Opened in 1931, they comprise some 30 different outdoor gardens and 10 vast exhibition greenhouses. Each garden represents a different climate, country or style, ranging from a collection of poisonous plants to gardens devoted to orchids or medicinal herbs. Nearby lies the Insectarium, in a bug-shape building. Its galleries are filled with all manner of displays and countless insects living and dead (and exotic butterflies in summer). Don't miss the gargantuan South

A tour aboard the botanical garden's mini-train (top left) takes in all the best sights including the Japanese Garden (top right), the Montréal–Shanghai Dream Lake Garden (bottom right), the Reception Gardens (bottom middle right), Lover's Bench (bottom left) and lots of exotic foliage (bottom middle left)

American cockroaches. In February visitors can try some high-protein morsels as local cooks whip up chocolate-covered ants, honey-dipped bees and the ever popular bug-centered lollipops.

Shanghai surprise The gardens' highlight is the 1991 2ha (6-acre) Montréal-Shanghai Dream Lake Garden, a perfect replica of one from the Ming dynasty (1368–1644) designed to celebrate the friendship between the two cities. Lakes, rocks and plants strive for a harmonious blend of yin and yang: small and large, soft and hard, light and dark, flowing and immovable. Look for the seven elegant pavilions, central reflecting pool, large rock-ery and collection of miniature trees known as "penjings" (on display in summer only). The Japanese Garden and Pavilion are exquisite as is the summer collection of bonsai trees.

THE BASICS

www.ville.montreal.qc.ca
/jardin
www.ville.montreal
qc.ca/insectarium
☐ F1
✉ Jardin Botanique: 4101
rue Sherbrooke Est;
Insectarium: 4581 rue
Sherbrooke Est
☎ Jardin Botanique: 514/
872–1400. L'Insectarium:
514/872–1400
🕐 Late Jun–early Sep
daily 9–6; early Sep–end
Oct 9–9; rest of year 9–5
🍴 Café
🚇 Viau, Pie IX 🚌 185
♿ Very good
💲 Expensive. Combined
ticket available (▷ 90,
Tips)
❓ Free shuttle bus from
Le Biodôme and Viau
Métro

More to See

CHÂTEAU DUFRESNE

www.chateaudufresne.qc.ca

Little in the symmetrical facade of this building suggests that it is actually two buildings, built between 1915 and 1918 for two brothers, Marius and Oscar Dufresne. Marius, the building's architect, lived in the west wing, his brother, a businessman who had grown rich producing shoes, lived in the east wing.

Created in a delightful Beaux Arts style, the house was modeled on the Petit-Trianon at Versailles, near Paris. When the Dufresne brothers and their families moved on, the house became a boys' school in the 1950s under the guardianship of Eudist priests, who covered many of the interior's racier friezes and murals to spare the blushes of their pupils.

Many of these murals have been recovered, along with much of the original interiors, offering a vivid insight into the lives of Montréal's French-speaking social elite at the beginning of the 20th century. A small exhibition places the house in context, but it is the sumptuous interiors that prove most compelling. Decadent marble staircases, gold-damask hangings, mahogany covered walls, stained-glass windows and beautiful coffered ceilings all catch the eye, along with the paintings, many by Guido Nincheri, an Italian artist who also decorated many of the city's churches.

🔲 F2 ✉ 2929 avenue Jeanne-d'Arc ☎ 514/259–9201 🕐 Thu–Sun 10–5 🚇 Pie-IX 🚻 Good 💷 Inexpensive

MAISONNEUVE

www.tourismemaisonneuve.qc.ca

Maisonneuve is the residential suburb to the south and east of the Parc Olympique, a formerly rundown but now partly regenerated district that owes its new lease of life to the 1976 Olympic Games. It began life as a model city, created by French-speaking citizens who felt they would be better off separated from the then predominantly Anglo-Saxon city of Montréal. For 35 years from 1883 it enjoyed its status as a self-contained city, and a degree of independent prosperity.

A Beaux Arts delight, Château Dufresne is just as sumptuous inside

Maisonneuve's ruling elite was influenced by the Utopian urban ideals of the time, and hoped to improve the civic, social and practical standing of the city's inhabitants by creating a model city. They commissioned wide boulevards and fine public buildings, many of them designed by Marius Dufresne, whose home, Château Dufresne (▷ 92), lies just beyond the Parc Maisonneuve.

Buildings worth a look include the Fire Station (4300 rue Notre-Dame Est), which owes a considerable architectural debt to Frank Lloyd Wright, the Beaux-Arts Marché Maisonneuve (▷ right) and the former public baths just opposite. Also eye-catching are the Théatre Denise Pelletier, near the junction of rue Morgan and Rue Sainte-Catherine Est, and the Église Très-Saint-Nom-de-Jésus. For all the city elders' good intentions, the devastating economic effects of the First World War and Depression brought an end to the city's prosperity and the city was incorporated into Montréal proper.

➕ H2 🚇 Pie-XI, Joliette, Viau

MARCHÉ MAISONNEUVE

The original Marché Maisonneuve, a magnificent Beaux Arts building dating from 1912 (notice the copper-plated main cupola and the château like towers), is now a cultural center, but farmers continue to sell their produce in this more modern building right next door. Flowers, pastries, local wine and cheese, and other traditional products can all be bought here. Other market products can be found at the more modern building nearby.

➕ H2 ✉ 4445 rue Ontario Est
☎ 514/937–7754 🕐 Mon–Wed, Sat 8–6, Thu–Fri 8–9, Sun 8–5 🚇 Pie-XI

PARC MAISONNEUVE

Parc Maisonneuve's slopes and frozen lakes provide a great spot for tobogganing, cross-country skiing and skating in winter. While in summer, the park is ideal for picnics, walking, cycling, and you can even play golf.

➕ E1 ✉ 4601 rue Sherbrooke Est and boulevard Pie-XI ☎ 514/872–6555 🕐 Daily 9am–10pm 🚇 Viau, Pie-IX 🅿 Good
🎫 Park free. Golf course moderate

Les Fête des enfants de Montréal *(Festival of Children)* in Maisonneuve Park

At the fringes of Montréal's Downtown core, and at the heart of the St. Lawrence River, are two islands and a variety of sights that are well worth making a special journey to visit.

Farther Afield and the Islands

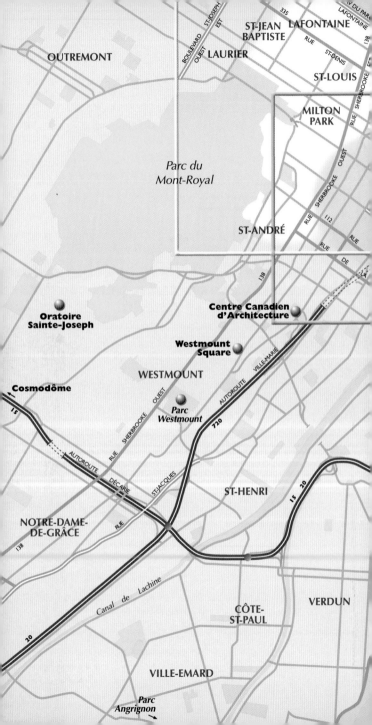

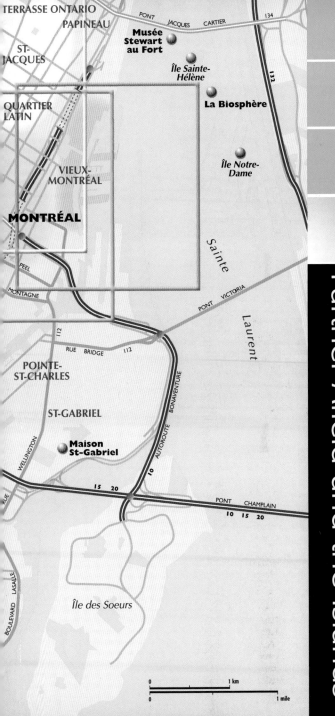

TERRASSE ONTARIO
PAPINEAU

ST-
JACQUES

QUARTIER
LATIN

VIEUX-
MONTRÉAL

MONTRÉAL

PEEL

MONTAGNE

POINTE-
ST-CHARLES

ST-GABRIEL

RUE

WELLINGTON

BOULEVARD LASALLE

PONT JACQUES CARTIER 134

**Musée
Stewart
au Fort**

*Île Sainte-
Hélène*

La Biosphère

*Île Notre-
Dame*

132

Sainte

Laurent

PONT VICTORIA

112

RUE BRIDGE 112

AUTOROUTE BONAVENTURE

10

**Maison
St-Gabriel**

15 20

PONT CHAMPLAIN

10 15 20

Île des Soeurs

0 1 km
0 1 mile

Farther Afield and the Islands

Centre Canadian d'Architecture

HIGHLIGHTS

● Façade
● Halls
● Mansion
● Conservatory
● Gardens

TIPS

● Guided tours in English are available on Thursday at 7.30pm and Saturday and Sunday at 1.30pm.
● Take the Saint-Mathieux exit at the Guy-Concordia métro stop for the quickest route to the Centre.

There's something fitting about the layout of what is arguably the world's premier architectural museum. Its U-plan fortress embraces an impressive 19th-century mansion built for one of Montréal's great plutocrats.

Temple of architecture The gray limestone facade is not terribly welcoming. Long and low, it is virtually windowless, and the front door, at the building's western end, appears an afterthought. But that door leads into six beautifully lighted halls given over to changing exhibits ranging from the academic to the whimsical—displays on modernist theory and American lawn culture are equally at home. Incorporated into the complex is the 1877 Shaughnessy Mansion, with its art nouveau conservatory, built for Canadian Pacific Railway

An amazing space provides the perfect setting for one of the world's most impressive architectural museums, displayed under beautiful lighting

chairman Sir Thomas Shaughnessy. Across the street, in a island of green between two busy main thoroughfares, is a garden designed by Melvin Charney, where fanciful fragments—a set of Doric columns here, a Victorian doorway there—tell the story of architecture.

Phyllis Lambert The woman behind all this is architect Phyllis Lambert. A defender of Montréal's architectural heritage, she founded the center in 1979 and presided, with architect Peter Rose, over the building of its present home (1985–89). She also contributed her own impressive collection— 65,000 prints and drawings (some by Leonardo da Vinci and Michelangelo), 50,000 architectural photographs and 180,000 books and publications dating from 15th-century manuscripts to the present. The archives are open by appointment.

THE BASICS

www.cca.qc.ca

🕂 D14

✉ 1920 rue Baile, between rues Saint-Marc and du Fort

☎ 514/939–7026

🕐 Wed–Sun 10–5, Thu 10–9

Ⓜ Guy-Concordia, Atwater

🚌 15, 150, 535

♿ Excellent

🖐 Centre moderate (free Thu 5.30–9). Sculpture Gardens free

❓ Excellent bookstore

Île Notre-Dame

Grand Prix of Canada, Parc Jean-Drapeau (left). Montréals' steel and glass casino (right)

THE BASICS

www.casinos-quebec.com

Off map at J11

Île Notre-Dame Casino: 1 avenue du Casino

Casino: 514/392–2746 or 800/665–2274 in Canada and US. Beach: 514/872-6211

Casino: daily 24 hours. Beach: Jun 23–Aug 27 daily 10–7 (if fine)

Jean-Drapeau

167 Les Îles (summer)

Summer ferry from Bassin Jacques-Cartier

Variable

Casino free. Beach moderate

Casino: visitors must be over 18; the wearing of shorts, leggings, T-shirts, sportwear, beachwear, running shoes and denim of any kind is not allowed

HIGHLIGHTS

● Beach
● Views
● Floral Park
● Casino

Before Expo '67, this thin island hugging the south shore of the St. Lawrence River didn't exist. Today it offers a huge variety of activities—car racing, swimming, and gambling—in addition to some magnificent views of the Montréal skyline.

Engineering feat When you bore a subway system through granite, you have to deposit all the rock you excavate. In the early 1960s Montréal's visionary mayor Jean Drapeau decided to drop it in the middle of the St. Lawrence River to create the venue for a world fair. He doubled the size of Île Sainte-Hélène (▷ opposite), and created a brand new island next to it. Now the two islands form the Parc Jean-Drapeau.

Attractions The most popular attraction on the island, and one of the most popular in the city, is the Casino de Montréal. Its owner, the Québec provincial government, has tried to re-create the glamour of a European gambling palace in two spectacular buildings, the former French and Québec Expo '67 pavilions. Apart from around 3,000 slot machines and 120 gaming tables, the casino houses five restaurants and a cabaret. The island's second-most popular attraction is the beach on the artificial lake. The island is also home to the Circuit Gilles-Villeneuve, the only Formula 1 racing track in North America and home of the Air Canada Grand Prix. A vast floral park, built for the Floralies Internationales festival in 1980, it is laced with canals and waterways, and filled with flowers, rose bushes and trees.

Rock climbing at Parc Jean-Drapeau (left)
La Ronde amusement park (right)

FARTHER AFIELD AND THE ISLANDS

★

TOP 25

Rustic calm meets urban energy on this lovely island in the middle of the St. Lawrence River. Its meadows and woodlands echo to the rattle of musket fire, the screams of roller-coaster riders and the music of open-air concerts.

Island to city park Two things transformed Île Sainte-Hélène from an isolated offshore green space into a vibrant city park: the building of the Jacques Cartier Bridge in 1930 between the island and the city; and Expo '67, which opened the island to the world. To prepare for it the city dumped tons of rubble from Métro excavations into the river to create space for pavilions, more than doubling the island's size.

Not just an island One of the fair's signature buildings—the geodesic dome that was the American pavilion—now encloses La Biosphère (▷ 104). Other Expo holdovers include La Ronde, the amusement park, bigger and better than in 1967, with one of the world's biggest roller-coasters; an open-air concert amphitheater; and Alexander Calder's metal sculpture, *Man*. An artificial lake is the setting for a summer-long fireworks competition. On the Cité du Havre peninsula opposite the island is Moshe Safdie's block modular housing known as Habitat '67 (▷ 36). The Old Fort was built by the British after the War of 1812. Its barracks from the Stewart Museum at the Fort and its parade square rattles to the drills of the Fraser Highlanders and Compagnie Franche de la Marine—two 18th-century rivals sharing one fort.

THE BASICS

www.parcjeandrapeau.com
J8
Île Sainte-Hélène
514/872–4537 or 514/872–6120; La Ronde 514/397–2000 or 800/361–4595
La Biosphère (▷ 104), Musée David-M-Stewart (▷ 106), Île Notre-Dame (▷ 100)
Jean-Drapeau
167 Les Îles (summer)
Quai Jacques-Cartier (514/281-8000 summer)

HIGHLIGHTS

● Parkland
● Views
● La Ronde
● Old Fort
● Fireworks competition

Oratoire Saint-Joseph

TOP 25

HIGHLIGHTS

● Oratory Museum
● The Primitive Chapel
● Joseph Guardo's eight bas-reliefs
● Gardens of the Way of the Cross

TIPS

● The Oratory Museum is open daily 10–5.
● The church has a good cafeteria and gift shop.
● You may hear the Petits Chanteurs choir at services on Saturday and Sunday.

The dome of the Oratoire Saint-Joseph, one of the world's largest, is a distinctive landmark on the Montréal skyline, and the church beneath it is the most important Roman Catholic shrine dedicated to Christ's earthly father.

Miracle cures The story of the Oratoire Saint-Joseph begins with Brother André Bessette, a diminutive, barely literate man born in 1837 to a poor rural family. He joined a religious order—the Congrégation du Saint-Croix—and worked as a porter in the order's Classical college at the foot of Mont-Royal. He built a small shrine to his favorite saint on the mountain slopes and cared for sick pilgrims. He developed an extraordinary reputation as a healer, and donations began to pour into the order from grateful pilgrims who wanted to help

Oratoire Saint-Joseph is a daunting landmark set against the dark night sky (right)
A statue of the famed healer, Brother Andre, beneath the dome in the apse (left)

André fulfill his dream of building a grand monument to St. Joseph. Construction began in 1924 and Brother André lived long enough to see the completion of the crypt, but the main church with its dome was not finished until 1937, long after his death.

Interior André was beatified in 1982 and buried in the oratory, which also includes part of his original chapel, a small museum about his life, the room in which he died (from a local hospice) and his preserved heart. The 56-bell carillon was originally cast for the Eiffel Tower but never installed. There are free carillon and organ recitals year-round. Be sure to climb to the observatory, one of Montréal's highest points, for a superb view, and to see the Carrara marble sculptures marking the Stations of the Cross in Mont-Royal.

THE BASICS

www.saint-joseph.org
🕂 Off map at A13
✉ 3800 chemin Queen Mary, near Côtes-des-Neiges
☎ 514/733–8211 or 877/672–8647
🕐 Daily late Jun–end Aug 6.30am–9.30pm; rest of year 7am–9pm
🍴 Café
Ⓜ Côte-des-Neiges
🚍 51, 144, 165, 166, 535 (peak hours)
♿ Very good
✋ Oratory free. Museum guided tours inexpensive

La Biosphère

Tour boats cruise past (left) the intricate structure of what is La Biosphère (right)

THE BASICS

www.biosphere.ec.gc.ca

🔢 J9

✉ 160 chemin du Tour-de-Île, Île Sainte-Hélène

☎ 514/283–5000

🕐 Late Jun–end Sep daily 10–6; early Oct–late Jun Mon, Wed, Thu, Fri 12–5, Sat, Sun and public hols 10–5

🚇 Jean-Drapeau

🚌 167 Les Îles (in summer)

♿ Very good

💰 Moderate

❓ Guided tours

HIGHLIGHTS

● River views
● Globe
● Water theater
● Satellite-fed data
● Interactive displays

There are two very good reasons for a visit to La Biosphère: to marvel at the shimmering geometric dome designed by Buckminster Fuller; and to see the center's fascinating interactive displays about the environment.

Masterpiece The Biosphère opened in 1995 but it is framed by what is left of one of Expo '67's most enduring architectural landmarks. When Expo opened, the glittering sphere that housed the US pavilion was the world's biggest geodesic structure and a popular attraction. Afterwards, it housed an aviary and was known as the world's largest bird cage. But in 1976 fire destroyed the dome's acrylic skin, reducing the proud structure to a corroding metal skeleton.

New role Displays inside highlight the ecosystems of the Great Lakes and St. Lawrence River, a network of waterways that not only provides a vital lifeline for trade, but whose shores are also home to nearly half of Canada's population. Tours open in the Discovery Hall, where an eye-catching 5m (16ft) globe helps explain the importance of water to our daily lives. In the Visions Hall, you enjoy views of the river and the city, while in the Connections Hall models, computers and diagrams demonstrate dramatically how we all share the same water as it falls as rain, runs through streams, is piped in and out of homes, and flows into the sea; you can also see the effect of pollution along the way. Take advantage of the soothing properties of water by bathing your feet.

More to See

COSMODÔME

www.cosmodome.org

The adventure of space exploration is the focus of this center. Exhibits include replicas of rockets and space ships, films, games, demonstrations.

➕ Off map ✉ 2150 Autoroute de Laurentides, Laval ☎ 514/978–3600 or 800/565–CAMP ⏰ Jun 24–Sep 1 daily 10–6; Sep 2–Jun 23 Tue–Sun 10–6 💰 Expensive

MAISON SAINT-GABRIEL

www.maisonsaint-gabriel.qc.ca

Saint Marguerite Bourgeoys ran a farm and school from this fine 17th-century farmhouse standing among Pointe-Saint-Charles tenements.

➕ F16 ✉ 2146 Place Dublin ☎ 514/935–8136 ⏰ Late Jun–early Sep Tue–Sun 11–6; Apr–late Jun, early Sep to mid-Dec Tue–Sun 1–5 🚇 Charlevoix 🚌 57 ♿ Good 💰 Moderate

PARC ANGRIGNON

This park has a small working farm, La Petite Ferme Angrignon.

➕ Off map at C17 ✉ 3400 boulevard des Trinitaires ☎ 514/872–3816; La Petite Ferme Angrignon 514/872–1400 ⏰ Park daily dawn to dusk. Farm early Jun–early Sep daily 9–5 🚇 Angrignon ♿ Good 💰 Free

PARC WESTMOUNT

Westmount contains playing fields, a conservatory and a good playground.

➕ A15 ✉ Rue Sherbrooke Ouest, between avenues Landsdowne and Melville ⏰ Daily 9am–dusk 🍴 Cafés nearby 🚇 Place Saint-Henri, Vendôme

MUSÉE STEWART AU FORT

www.stewart-museum.org

Collections of firearms, scientific instruments and domestic items.

➕ J8 ✉ Le Fort, Île Sainte-Hélène ☎ 514/861–6701 ⏰ Mid-May to early Sep daily 10–5; early Sep to mid-May Wed–Mon 10–5 🚇 Île Sainte-Hélène 🚌 167 ♿ Poor 💰 Moderate. Joint ticket with La Biosphère

WESTMOUNT SQUARE

Black-metal and tinted-glass master-piece by the modernist architect Ludwig Mies van der Rohe (1964).

➕ B14 ✉ Rue Sainte-Catherine Ouest 🚇 Atwater

Maison Saint-Gabriel, dating back to 1668, is now a heritage museum

Where to Stay

Whether you like to stay in the thick of it or prefer some peace and quiet, or require large chain hotels rather than a more intimate establishment, Montréal can satisfy all tastes.

Introduction

Montréal has a wide range of high-quality accommodation, from boutique hotels in the old port area to glittering luxury places in the Downtown and Mont-Royal districts.

Where to Stay

The most charming area to stay is Vieux-Montréal, where around a dozen intimate and interesting hotels in the mid- and luxury ranges offer accommodation close to the city's main historic sights. If you prefer to be nearer to the best shopping, or want a larger, international or chain hotel, then the best bet is Downtown, which is still convenient for sightseeing. Budget hotels are relatively thin on the ground, except in the Quartier Latin and around, though here the location, while good for nightlife and dining options, is far less appealing. Places near the bus station, in particular, are best avoided.

Best to Book

Although Montréal has plenty of accommodation, with more hotels opening every year, the city's increasing popularity with visitors means that it can still be difficult to secure a place to stay in high season and other busy times. Always book well ahead if you plan to visit from mid-May to September, in the busy shopping weeks before Christmas, or during popular events. Try contacting the visitor center for last-minute and other options. Or consider staying in one of the city's many bed-and-breakfasts, though these can be some way from the city hub.

SAVING MONEY

Smaller hotels often have a variety of rooms at different prices, so don't assume the first room you are offered is the cheapest. Few hotels will offer bargains in peak times, but the rest of the time you may be able to find up to 50 percent off the listed price. Hotels that cater predominantly to businesspeople often offer discounted weekend rates. Many hotels also offer discounted rates online and reductions for stays of two, three or more days. Always ask what is included in a rate, especially breakfasts.

Whether you stay at a large chain hotel or a smaller individual one, you are sure to receive a warm welcome

Budget Hotels

PRICES

Expect to pay up to $130 for a budget hotel

AUBERGE DE JEUNESSE YOUTH HOSTEL

www.hostellingmontreal.com
Superior hostel with 15 private rooms and 243 dormitory-style beds.
D13 ⊠ 1030 rue Mackay ☎ 514/843–3317 or 866/843–3317 ⓠ Lucien l'Allier

HÔTEL LORD BERRI

www.lordberri.com
Good modern hotel with 154 rooms near the Université du Québec à Montréal and rue Saint-Denis.
F10 ⊠ 1199 rue Berri ☎ 514/845–9236 or 800/361–0363 ⓠ Berri-UQAM

HÔTEL MANOIR SHERBROOKE

www.armormanoir.com
Converted Victorian building with 22 pleasant rooms. Continental breakfast included.
D9 ⊠ 157 rue Sherbrooke Est ☎ 514/845–0915 or 800/203–5485 ⓠ Sherbrooke

HÔTEL MARITIME PLAZA

www.hotelmaritime.com
A favorite with bus tours, this hotel is convenient for shops and museums. 241 rooms and suites.
D13 ⊠ 1155 rue Guy ☎ 514/932–1411 or 800/363–6255 ⓠ Guy Concord, Lucien L'Allier

HÔTEL LE ROBERVAL

www.leroberval.com
No-frills hotel with 43 rooms and suites near downtown.
F9 ⊠ 505 boulevard René-Lévesque Est ☎ 514/286–5215 ⓠ Champ-de-Mars

HÔTEL LE ST-ANDRÉ

www.hotelstandre.ca
Charming 62-room hotel close to Vieux-Montréal and the Quartier Latin.
F9 ⊠ 1285 rue Saint-André ☎ 514/849–7070 or 800/265–7071 in Canada and the US ⓠ Berri-UQAM

MCGILL UNIVERSITY

www.mcgill.ca/residences
During the long summer recess (mid-May to Aug), visitors can rent student lodgings at McGilll University—more than 1,000 rooms. These are inexpensive, right in the city center, in a pleasant

BED-AND-BREAKFAST

B&B options can be booked through tourist offices and the following agency:
Bed and Breakfast Downtown Network
www.bbmontreal.ca
⊠ 3458 avenue Laval ☎ 514/289–9749 or 800/267–5180

Good websites for bed-and-breakfast in Montréal include www.bedandbreakfast.com/montreal and www.canadianbandbguide.ca

campus setting and include use of the university gym, pool and other facilities. Some rooms have access to kitchenettes, but most have shared bathroom facilities.
D11 ⊠ 3935 rue University ☎ 514/398–6367 ⓠ McGill

QUALITY HOTEL DOWNTOWN

www.qualityhoteldowntownmontreal.com
This 140-room hotel's location close to McGill University makes it popular with visiting students and parents.
D10 ⊠ 3440 avenue du Parc Avenue ☎ 514/849–1413 or 800/228–5151 ⓠ Place-des-Arts

LA RÉSIDENCE DU VOYAGEUR

www.hotelresidencevoyager.com
Close to the attractions of the Quartier Latin and the Plateau Mont-Royal, this hotel has 28 comfortable rooms. Breakfast is included in the room rate.
F8 ⊠ 847 rue Sherbrooke Est ☎ 514/527–9515 ⓠ Sherbrooke

YWCA

www.ydesfemmesmtl.org
Simple rooms (63) for single, double and multiple occupancy. Women have access to YWCA health facilities.
D13 ⊠ 1355 boulevard René-Lévesque Quest ☎ 514/866–9942 ⓠ Lucien L'Allier

Mid-Range Hotels

PRICES

Expect to pay between $130 and $250 for a mid-range hotel

AUBERGE BONAPARTE

www.bonaparte.com
This delightful 31-room inn in the heart of Vieux-Montréal has views of the Basilique Notre-Dame gardens next door.
✚ F11 ✉ 447 rue Saint-Françoise-Xavier ☎ 514/844-1448 Ⓜ Place d'Armes

AUBERGE DE LA FONTAINE

www.aubergedelafontaine.com
With just 18 rooms and three suites, this intimate hotel near a bicycle path faces Parc Lafontaine in the trendy Plateau Mont-Royal district. It is a welcoming little inn with vivid but appealing decoration and a good breakfast included in the room rate.
✚ D7 ✉ 1301 rue Rachel Est ☎ 514/597-0166 or 800/597-0597 Ⓜ Mont-Royal

AUBERGE LE JARDIN D'ANTOINE

www.hotel-jardin-antoine.qc.ca
Reproduction antiques lend a charming period feel to this 25-room hotel at the heart of the rue Saint-Denis and Quartier Latin nightlife and entertainment district.
✚ E9 ✉ 2024 rue Saint-Denis ☎ 514/843-4506 or 800/361-4506 Ⓜ Berri-UQAM

AUBERGE DE LA PLACE ROYALE

www.aubergeplaceroyale.com
A superior bed-and-breakfast in a fine 19th-century Vieux-Port building, with nine moderate rooms and three suites, filled with antiques, and (from the most expensive rooms) views of the waterfront. The other rooms look onto a back street.
✚ G11 ✉ 115 rue de la Commune Ouest ☎ 514/287-0522 Ⓜ Place-d'Armes

BEST WESTERN EUROPA CENTRE-VILLE

www.europahotelmtl.com
The excellent downtown location and good selection of restaurants here distinguish this 184-room hotel.
✚ D12 ✉ 1240 rue Drummond ☎ 514/866-6492 or 800/361-3000 Ⓜ Peel, Guy-Concordia

RESERVATIONS

Although greater Montréal has some 23,000 hotel beds, advance reservations are advisable, particularly from May to August. Even if you guarantee your booking with a credit card, reconfirm a few days ahead. Receptionists are usually bilingual in French and English. If you arrive without accommodations, the city's tourist offices will help you to find a room.

CHÂTEAU VERSAILLES

www.versailleshotels.com
This has become one of the city's most elegant hotels with 65 rooms and suites. Many rooms have fireplaces.
✚ C13 ✉ 1659 rue Sherbrooke Ouest ☎ 514/933-3611 or 888/933-8111 Ⓜ Guy-Concordia

DELTA MONTRÉAL

www.deltamontrealcom
A fine 456-room high-rise chain hotel, with pleasant rooms that offer views over Downtown or to Mont-Royal, and are convenient for all the central sights. Use of excellent exercise and swimming facilities.
✚ D11 ✉ 475 avenue du President-Kennedy ☎ 514/286-1986 or 877/286-1986 Ⓜ McGill, Place-des-Arts

FAIRMONT LA REINE ELIZABETH

www.fairmont.com
This large and long-established hotel has over 1,000 rooms and suites, and sits above the main railway station. It is the hotel in which John Lennon and Yoko staged their famous "bed-in" in 1969. Excellent modern rooms and service, especially on the special "Gold Floor."
✚ E12 ✉ 900 boulevard René-Lévesque Ouest ☎ 514/861-3511 or 800/441-1414 Ⓜ Bonaventure

HÔTEL DE L'INSTITUT
www.ithq.qc.ca
Top civil servants love this 42-room hotel on the top floors of Québec's best hotel training school, right in the Quartier Latin.
🚑 E9 ✉ 3535 rue Saint-Denis ☎ 514/282–5120 or 800/361–5111 🚇 Sherbrooke

HÔTEL DE LA MONTAGNE
www.hoteldelamontagne.com
There are 135 spacious rooms, a good restaurant, a rooftop terrace and pool.
🚑 D12 ✉ 1430 rue de la Montagne ☎ 514/288–5656 or 800/361–6262 🚇 Peel

HÔTEL NELLIGAN
www.hotelnelligan.com
A beautiful and romantic hotel in an 1850s converted building, with 35 rooms and 28 suites. In a perfect Vieux-Montréal spot close to the Basilique Notre-Dame.
🚑 F11 ✉ 106 rue Saint-Paul Ouest ☎ 514/788–2040 or 877/788–2040 🚇 Place-d'Armes

HÔTEL PLACE D'ARMES
www.hotelplacedarmes.com
Occupying a beautiful old building, many of the 44 elegantly furnished rooms have ornate carvings.
🚑 F11 ✉ 701 place d'Armes ☎ 514/842–1887 or 888/450–1887 🚇 Place d'Armes

LE MARRIOTT CHÂTEAU CHAMPLAIN
www.marriott.com
The best rooms in this 36-story chain hotel, popular with business travellers, look through the building's distinctive half-moon windows over Place du Canada. Well-located for access to the Underground City.
🚑 D13 ✉ 1050 rue de la Gauchetière Ouest ☎ 514/878–9000 or 800/200–5909 🚇 Bonaventure

LE NOUVEL HÔTEL
www.lenouvelhotel.com
This modern, functional hotel, with 175 rooms, is in a convenient location.
🚑 D13 ✉ 1740 boulevard René-Lévesque Ouest ☎ 514/931–8841 or 800/363–6063 🚇 Guy-Concordia

OMNI MONTRÉAL
www.omnihotels.com
Excellent service and 300 fine rooms, many with lovely views out over Mont-Royal.
🚑 D11 ✉ 1050 Sherbrooke Ouest ☎ 514/284–1110 or 800/843–6664 🚇 Peel

LES PASSANTS DU SANS SOUCY
www.lesanssoucy.com
You can't miss the entrance to this delightful inn with nine rooms and one suite, as it is a functioning art gallery.
🚑 F11 ✉ 171 rue Saint-Paul Ouest ☎ 514/842–2634 🚇 Square-Victoria, Place d'Armes

LE SAINT-SULPICE
www.lesaintsulpice.com
A good location—right by the Basilique Notre-Dame —is the main draw of this 108-room hotel, opened in 2002 in a modern building designed to blend with its period surroundings.
🚑 F11 ✉ 414 rue Saint-Sulpice ☎ 514/288–1000 or 877/785–7423 🚇 Place-d'Armes

SOFITEL MONTRÉAL
www.sofitel.com
Modern skyscraper hotel with 241 bright, spacious rooms and stylish interiors. Convenient for the Musée des Beaux-Arts, Musée McGill and the southern areas of Downtown.
🚑 D12 ✉ 1155 rue Sherbrooke Ouest ☎ 514/285–9000 or 877/285–9001 🚇 Peel

---

HIDDEN COSTS

So as not to have a nasty shock on checking out of your hotel, it is worth knowing the various taxes and other hidden charges that will appear on Montréal bills. Some hotels will include these charges in the published room rate: most will not. The additions include the country-wide Goods and Services Tax (GST) at seven percent and a provincial sales tax of 7.5 percent. There is also a more negligible city tax of just under $3. Hotels will also often charge high rates for any direct-dial calls made from your room.

Luxury Hotels

BONAVENTURE HILTON INTERNATIONAL

www.hilton.com
Astride the downtown Bonaventure exhibition center, this 360-room, luxury hotel has an all-season outdoor pool and extensive rooftop gardens.
✚ E12 ✉ 1 place Bonaventure ☎ 514/878–2332 or 800/445–8667 in Canada, 800/ HILTONS in US Ⓜ Bonaventure

LE CENTRE SHERATON

www.sheraton.com/lecentre
The huge lobby of this 825-room business hotel is full of greenery.
✚ D13 ✉ 1201 boulevard René-Lévesque Ouest ☎ 514/878–2000 Ⓜ Bonaventure, Peel

HÔTEL LE GERMAIN

www.hotelgermain.com
Ultra-chic boutique hotel close to museums and downtown. 101 rooms.
✚ E12 ✉ 2050 rue Mansfield ☎ 514/849–2050 or 877/333–2050 Ⓜ McGill

HÔTEL GODIN

www.hotelgodin.com
One of the city's newest and most striking hotels—opened 2004—starkly contemporary in design and convenient for the nightlife of the Quartier Latin. 136 rooms and 12 suites.
✚ E10 ✉ 10 rue Sherbrooke Ouest ☎ 514/843–6000 or 866/744–6346 Ⓜ Saint-Laurent

HÔTEL INTERCONTINENTAL MONTRÉAL

www.intercontinental.com
Near to Vieux-Montréal, this luxury hotel has 357 rooms, a health club and a swimming pool.
✚ F11 ✉ 360 rue Saint-Antoine Ouest ☎ 514/987–9900 or 800/361–3600 Ⓜ Square-Victoria

HÔTEL ST-PAUL

www.hotelstpaul.com
Choose between airy white "sky rooms," with large windows, and "earth rooms" in warmer shades at this designer boutique hotel on the southern edge of Vieux-Montréal.

CHILDREN

Some hotels have family-plan deals that allow children sharing a room with their parents to stay (and sometimes eat) free. Most have rooms equipped with two double beds and some provide a third, smaller bed in the same room for a modest fee. More expensive hotels may offer child-minding services and children's programs. Swimming pools and in-room electronic games and movies also make some hotels particularly child-friendly.

Also known for its celebrated Cube restaurant. 96 rooms and 24 suites.
✚ F12 ✉ 355 rue McGill ☎ 514/380–2222 or 866/380–2202 Ⓜ Square-Victoria

LOEWS HÔTEL VOGUE

www.loewshotels.com
Bathrooms in the 154 rooms of this fashionable downtown hotel all have whirlpool baths, televisions and phones.
✚ D12 ✉ 1425 rue de la Montague ☎ 514/285–5555 or 800/465–6654 Ⓜ Peel, Guy-Concordia

PIERRE-DU-CALVERT

www.pierreducalvert.ca
In an 18th-century building in Vieux-Montréal with nine sumptuously decorated rooms. Fine restaurant.
✚ G10 ✉ 405 rue Bonsecours ☎ 514/282–1725 Ⓜ Champ-de-Mars

RITZ-CARLTON MONTRÉAL

www.ritzcarlton.com
Stately and fashionable Edwardian hotel, with 185 rooms and 45 suites.
✚ C12 ✉ 1228 rue Sherbrooke Ouest ☎ 514/842–4212 or 800/363–0366 Ⓜ Peel

W MONTRÉAL

www.whotels.com
Chic, modern design, Bliss spas and a "whatever, whenever" approach to service. 152 rooms and 30 suites.
✚ E12 ✉ 901 Square-Victoria ☎ 514/395–3100 Ⓜ Square-Victoria

Here is key information to help smooth your path both before you go and when you arrive. Get savvy with the local transport, explore the Montréal websites or check out what festivals are taking place.

Planning Ahead

When to Go

The best time to visit Montréal is between late May and late October. The summer from the end of June to the first weekend in September is rich in festivals. Autumn brings cooler weather better for walking; the parks can be spectacular. In winter, a visit can be coupled with a trip to a ski resort.

TIME

Montréal operates on Eastern Standard Time, 3 hours ahead of Los Angeles, 5 hours behind London.

AVERAGE DAILY MAXIMUM TEMPERATURES

JAN	FEB	MAR	APR	MAY	JUN	JUL	AUG	SEP	OCT	NOV	DEC
18°F	20°F	31°F	45°F	63°F	73°F	79°F	77°F	69°F	56°F	43°F	33°F
-8°C	-7°C	-1°C	7°C	17°C	23°C	26°C	25°C	21°C	13°C	6°C	1°C

Spring (April to May) The leap between winter and summer can be very abrupt. It is also the least attractive time of year as the melting snow reveals dead grass littered with the debris of winter.

Summer (June to August) begins on June 24, the date of the Québec Fête National. The city can be very hot and humid, especially in downtown.

Autumn (September to October), with cooler temperatures and sunny days, makes for ideal exploring. There are fewer visitors, so you can see the city as the locals do.

Winter (November to March), Montréal's defining season, can be brutally cold, with occasional blizzards that shut down the city. There's often a brief thaw in January.

WHAT'S ON

January/February *Fête des Neiges*: Celebrations on Île Notre-Dame and Sainte-Hélène.

March *St. Patrick's Day Parade*.

April–September *Baseball season* Montréal Expos.

May *Festival de Théâtre des Ameriques*: New drama.

June *Festival du Nouveau Cinéma*: Independent and avant-garde films/videos.

International Fireworks Competition: Thu and Sun (mid-June to mid-July).

Grand Prix du Canada: Formula 1 on Île Notre-Dame.

Tour d'Île: 40,000 bicyclists try this 66km (41-mile) trek through the city streets.

Fête Vieux-Port: Concerts, dancing and other entertainment through the first Mon in September.

Mozart Plus: Montréal Symphony Orchestra concerts in Basilique Notre-Dame.

Fringe Festival: Theater, dance and music.

July *International Jazz Festival*: Largest celebration of jazz in the world.

Juste Pour Rire: The world's largest comedy festival.

Nuits d'Afrique: Traditional African music and festivities on boulevard Saint-Laurent.

Franco Folies: 1,000 musicians in a celebration of French songs and music.

August *Omnium du Maurier*: International tennis.

Les Fêtes Gourmandes Internationales de Montréal: Sample world foods.

Festival des Films du Monde: World film festival.

September–May *L'Opéra de Montréal*: The opera season.

Useful Websites

www.montrealplus.ca
This broad travel guide provides information about Montréal lodging, dining, shopping and entertainment.

www.vieux.montreal.qc.ca
A comprehensive guide to historic Vieux-Montréal. Includes live webcams, maps and historical information and tours.

www.canada.com/montreal
News and features from the *Montréal Gazette*, the city's daily newspaper.

www.tourisme-montreal.org
You can download maps, print itineraries and read up on attractions and coming events on this, the official tourist information website for Montréal.

www.montrealjazzfest.com
Every year some 2,000 jazz musicians perform more than 500 shows in Montréal's largest festival, the Festival International de Jazz de Montréal. This site includes a venue map, ticket information and performer news.

www.hahaha.com
The Just for Laughs comedy festival propelled performers such as Jerry Seinfeld and Ray Romano to comedy stardom. The site has news of this year's festival and ticket information.

www.parcjeandrapeau.com
The site of Expo '67, Park Jean-Drapeau is an island jewel surrounded by the Saint Lawrence River. You can browse for information on tourist attractions, events, services, maps and history.

www.menumontreal.net
With more than 5,000 places to eat, Montréal is arguably the restaurant capital of Canada. You can narrow your search for the perfect meal by keyword or district on this funky restaurant site.

PRIME TRAVEL SITES

www.fodors.com
A complete travel-planning site. You can research prices and weather; book air tickets, cars and rooms; ask questions (and get answers) from fellow travelers; and find links to other sites.

www.montreal.com
Exhaustive lists of what to do, and where to sleep and eat. You'll find information for all tastes from tourist sights to local activities.

INTERNET CAFÉS

There are Internet cafés at the main visitor center and railway and bus stations. A full list of Internet cafés can be found at www.pagesjaunes.ca

Atwater Library and Computer Centre
www.atwaterlibrary.ca
A center with PCs and Macs. No food.
🚇 E9 ✉ 1200 avenue Atwater ☎ 514/935-7344 🕐 Mon, Wed 10–8, Tue, Thu, Fri 10–6, Sat 10–5 💵 $4 per hour

Getting There

FLYING TIMES

Airport gate to airport gate, Montréal is about an hour by air from New York City; three hours from Chicago; four hours 30 minutes from Dallas; six hours from Los Angeles; six hours from London; and 22 hours from Sydney.

ARRIVING BY CAR

Montréal is 47km (29 miles) from the US border, and is accessed from New York City on the New York State Thruway (I-87), which in Canada becomes Route 15. Or you can take US I-89 north until it becomes Route 133 that then becomes Highway 133, a road that leads straight to the heart of Montréal's Downtown. Coming from Massachusetts, follow I-91, and then pick up Route 55 and Route 10 through the Eastern Townships area to Montréal. From Boston, take I-93, I-89 and Route 133. If coming from elsewhere in Canada, use the Trans-Canada Highway (Highway 1), which crosses the south-ern flanks of the city as Route 20, with a spur, Route 720 that connects to the city. The main roads from Toronto and Ottawa are Routes 401 and 417 respectively. Both con-verge west of the Montréal, where you can pick up Route 20 or 40 for travel to the city.

AIRPORTS

Montréal has two airports. Montréal-Trudeau is 22.5km (14 miles) southwest of the city and handles commercial flights; Aéroport de Mirabel is 56km (35 miles) northwest of the city and handles charter flights.

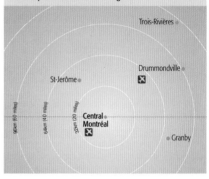

ARRIVING BY AIR

Montréal's main airport for international and domestic flights is the Aéroport International Pierre-Elliott-Trudeau de Montréal (✉ 975 boulevard Roméo-Vachon Nord, Dorval; ☎ 514/394–7377; flight information toll-free in Canada 800/465–1213; www.admtl.com). It is more commonly known as Montréal-Trudeau or by its previous name, Dorval, or Aéroport de Montréal-Dorval, after its nearest town. Its international airport code is YUL. Considerable rebuilding at the airport was mostly completed in 2006, creating a new international arrivals area and Transborder Zone for visitors to and from the United States.

FROM THE ÁEROPORT MONTRÉAL-TRUDEAU

If you are on a tight budget, then it is possible to use public transportation to reach the city, though it is a slow and complicated process involving several changes of bus and/or subur-ban trains. Allow 60–90 minutes. Much easier, and far more popular, is to use the dedicated L'Aérobus shuttle (☎ 514/842–2281, www.autobus.qc.ca), which runs from the air-port in front of the main terminal building to

the main bus station (Station Centrale Berri ☒ 505 boulevard de Maisonneuve). En route it stops at three city hotels: the Sheraton, Château Champlain and Fairmont La Reine Elizabeth. Services depart every 25 minutes, with the first departure from the airport at 7am and the last at 2am. The first service from

the bus station is at 4.05am, the last at 11pm. Tickets can be obtained from the airport or bus-station ticket kiosks. The cost is $13 one-way, $22.75 return, with reductions for senior citizens and children between 5 and 12. Children under 5 travel free. Journey time is about 35–45 minutes, depending on traffic. Free minibus shuttles run from the bus station to around 40 Downtown, Vieux-Montréal and Quartier-Latin hotels, but check to see if you wouldn't be better off disembarking from the main Aérobus shuttle earlier and walking directly to your hotel. Places can be pre-booked by calling ☎ 514/843–4938.

Taxis charge a set fare of $35 (plus any tip) from the airport to central Downtown locations from the Vieux-Montréal district to near avenue Les Pins, between Atwater and Papineau.

ARRIVING BY TRAIN

Canadian trains run by VIA Rail (☎ 514/989–2626 or 888/842–7245 in Québec; www.viarail.ca) and US trains operated by Amtrak (☎ 800/872–7245; www.amtrak.com) all arrive at Montréal's main railway station, the Gare Centrale (Central Station), behind the Fairmont La Reine Elizabeth hotel at 895 rue de la Gauchetière Ouest. The station is at the heart of Downtown, connected to the Underground City at several points, and to the Bonaventure Métro station.

ARRIVING BY BUS

Montréal's Station Centrale d'Autobus at 505 boulevard de la Maisonneuve (☎ 514/842–22810) has connections to the Berri-UQAM Métro station. It handles all Greyhound (www. greyhound.ca) and other long-distance bus services from other Canadian and some US cities, including Orléans Express (www.orleansexpress.com) that covers most routes in Québec province, and Voyageur (www.voyageur.com), which has services to Ottawa and elsewhere. The quickest buses to Québec City and Ottawa take 2 hours 20 minutes. Buses from New York take eight hours and seven hours from Boston.

Getting Around

TRAVEL INSURANCE

Travel insurance, including coverage for medical costs, is strongly recommended. Check your insurance coverage and buy a supplementary policy as needed.

VISITORS WITH DISABILITIES

Montréal's Métro system is not adapted for wheelchairs. There are no elevators and the escalators are not always dependable, so deep stations such as Snowdon and Lucien-L'Allier are difficult for anyone with mobility problems. The new, low-slung buses are a little better. Passengers with a cane or crutches can embark with care. They also accept wheelchairs at the rear exit doors, but space is limited and the entrance tight. Most major attractions and hotels are much better with ramps and elevators, and facilities to help hearing- and vision-impaired visitors. For additional information contact Kéroul ✉ 4545 avenue Pierre-De Coubertin, Box 1000, Branch M, Montréal, H1V 3R2 ☎ 514/252-3104; www.keroul.qc.ca.

Montréal has 169 bus routes and a Métro system with 65 stations and links to more than 32km (20 miles) of walkways in the Underground City (☎ 514/786-4636; www.stcum.qc.ca). There are four color-coded lines (green, orange, blue and yellow). You can buy flat-fare one-way tickets, either as singles or in a discounted six-ticket strip called a carnet at Métro booths and some retail outlets, but not on buses. Tickets are good on both the Métro and the buses, but if you have to change from one to the other, get a transfer (une correspondence in French) from your bus driver or from the machine in the Métro station where your journey started. Weekly and monthly passes are available. Bus passengers with no ticket, pass, or transfer must have the exact fare.

The orange and green lines operate Monday to Friday 5.30am-12.30am, Saturday 5.30am-1am, Sunday 5.30am-12.30am. The blue line runs daily between 5.30am-12.15am. Most buses run until around 12.30am, when a night service takes over on 20 routes. The yellow line runs 5.30am-1am Monday to Friday and Sunday, and 5.30am-1.30am on Saturday.

ROUTES AND TICKETS

● Contact STCUM (Société de Transport de la Communauté Urbaine de Montréal)
✉ Mezzanine Level, Berri-UQAM Métro Station
☎ 514/786-4636; www.stcum.qc.ca
🕐 Mon-Fri 7.30am-8.30pm, Sat-Sun, public hols 8.30-4.30

MÉTRO AND BUS SERVICES

● Four key stations provide the main interchanges between lines: Berri-UQAM (orange, green and yellow lines); Lionel Groulx (green and orange); Snowdon (blue and orange); Jean-Talon (blue and orange).
● A one-day or three-day tourist pass—Carte touristique (Tourist Card)—allows you to travel at will on buses or Métro. Further information ☎ 514/280-5507. Both may be purchased

from the tourist office or downtown hotels.
● A transfer system allows you to complete a
Métro journey by bus (and vice versa) at no
extra cost. A transfer ticket (*correspondance*) is
available from machines in the Métro, and
valid for 90 minutes. Bus-to-bus or bus-to-
Métro transfers can be obtained from drivers
as you board a bus. However, Métro transfers
cannot be used to gain re-entry to the Métro.
● The STCUM also operates two commuter
train lines. One, leaving from Gare Windsor
and the Vendôme Métro station, runs as far
west as Hudson and Regaud. The other runs
north from Gare Centrale to Deux-Montagnes.
Weekend service is sparse. Tickets can be
purchased from machines at stations, but all
STCUM passes are good for travel within Zone
1 on both lines. Fares are based on the distance traveled.

TAXIS

Taxis stand outside main hotels, near the rail-
way station and at major intersections, and can
be hailed on the street.
Cab companies include:
● Co-op ☎ 725–9885
● Diamond ☎ 273–6331
● La Salle ☎ 277–2552
A 10–15 per cent tip is normal.

CAR RENTAL

To rent a car in Montréal you must be 25 or
over (21 if using a major credit card).
● Avis ✉ 1225 rue Metcalfe
☎ 514/866–7906 or 800/321–3652
● Budget ✉ 1240 rue Guy ☎ 514/937–9121,
514/866–7675 (main train station) or
800/268–8900
● Hertz Canada ✉ 1073 rue Drummond
☎ 514/938–1717 or 800/263–0600 (English),
800/263–0678 (French)
● Thrifty-Québec ✉ 845 rue Sainte-Catherine
Est ☎ 514/845–5954 or 800/847–4389.
● National ✉ 1200 rue Stanley
☎ 514/878–2771 or 800/387–4747

WATERWAY TRANSPORT

Even if you don't use
Montréal's ferries as a practical means of transport, it's
worth taking a boat just to
see some of the city from the
river. Navettes Maritimes du
St-Laurent (☎ 514/281–8000
or 866/228–3280; www.
navettesmaritimes.com) runs
ferries from the Vieux-Port to
the Réal Bouvier Marina in
Longueuil. Boats leave hourly
from May to mid-Oct starting
at 10.35am from Montréal
and returning from Longueuil
11am–7pm (except 9.35am–
10.35pm and 11am–11pm
Fri–Sat late Jun–early Sep).

TOURIST OFFICES

Montréal's main tourist office
is the:
Centre Infotouriste
www.bonjourquebec.com
✉ 1001 Square-Dorchester
☎ 514/873–2015 or
877/266–5687 in Canada and
the US ◷ Jun 1–Labor Day
daily 7am–8pm; Labor
Day–May 31 daily 9–6
Ⓜ Peel

There is a smaller tourist
information office in Vieux-
Montréal
✉ 174 rue Notre-Dame Est
at Place Jacques-Cartier
☎ 514/873–2015
◷ Jun 1–Labor Day
Wed–Sun 7am–8pm; Labor
Day–May 31 9–6

Essential Facts

Check your visa and passport requirements before leaving home:
www.britishembassy.gov.uk
www.britainusa.com

MONEY

US dollars are widely accepted; for the best exchange rate use a bank or currency exchange office. ATM cards are widely accepted. French speakers sometimes call a penny a "sou," the nickel "cinq sous" and the quarter "vingt-cinq sous." English speakers call the dollar coin a "looney" after the bird (a loon) on its obverse and the bimetal $2 coin a "tooney."

5 dollars

10 dollars

50 dollars

100 dollars

ELECTRICITY
● Current in Canada is 100 volts AC (60Hz). Plug adaptors are needed to match the two-prong sockets.

MAIL
● Montréal's main post office is Postes Canada ✉ 1025 rue University ☎ 888/550–6333; www.canadapost.ca Ⓑ Bonaventure
● Smaller post offices are inside shops, department stores and train stations wherever there are Postes Canada signs.
● Stamps can be bought from post offices, the Centre Infotouriste in Square-Dorchester, train station and bus terminals, airports and convenience stores.
● Within Canada, postcards and letters up to 30g are 51¢; up to 100g, $1.05; up to 500g, $2.49. Cards and letters to the US cost £1.49 up to 30g. Rates for other destinations are $1.25 up to 30g and $2.10 from 30 to 50g.
● Letters sent poste restante should be sent to the main post office marked "c/o General Delivery" or "c/o Poste Restante." State a collection date if possible, otherwise letters will be returned to the sender after 15 days. Take photo identification (e.g. passport, driver's license) when collecting mail. Letters sent for collection in hotels should be marked "Guest Mail, Hold for Arrival."

OPENING HOURS
● Shops: Mon–Fri 9 or 9.30–6, Sat 9–5. Some shops open Sun 12–5. Some stores open longer hours Thu–Fri 10–9, Sat 10–6, Sun 12–5.
● Banks: Mon–Fri 9–4. Some larger banks open Sat morning.
● Post offices: Mon–Fri 8.30–5.30. Some open Sat mornings.

PUBLIC HOLIDAYS
● January 1; Good Friday; Easter Monday; Victoria Day (Monday in mid-May); Fête Nationale (June 24); Canada Day (July 1);

Labor Day; Thanksgiving; Remembrance Day; December 25; December 26.

SALES TAX

● You can reclaim GST (Goods and Services Tax) on accommodation and for goods taken out of the country (purchases must total at least $200, and each receipt must show a minimum total of £50.).

● Keep receipts and complete the Goods and Services Tax Refund for Visitors form available at retailers, duty free shops or Revenue Canada.

● You can apply for a TVQ (Québec Sales Tax) rebate (goods and services) on the same form.

TELEPHONES

● Local calls from phone booths cost 25¢. This includes calls to all numbers in the 514 area code—all municipalities on the island of Montréal itself—and to some numbers in the surrounding 450 area code (in such off-island suburbs as Laval, Longueuil and Brossard).

● For a number outside the area you are in, including all toll-free numbers, dial 1, then the area code.

● For international and long-distance calls, buy a phone card, or find public phones that accept credit cards.

● Direct dial phones are common in many hotels and motels. A surcharge is levied.

● Many organizations have toll-free numbers—800, 888, or 877 prefix. Some operate within a province, others in Canada, and a few from North America.

● Information for local numbers can be reached by dialing 411.

● To call the US from Canada dial the area code and the number.

● To call the UK from Canada dial 011 44, followed by the area code (minus its first zero), and the number required.

● To call Canada from the US dial 1, the area code, and then the number.

● To call Canada from the UK dial 001, then the area code, and then the number.

USEFUL NUMBERS

American Express
☎ 1-800/869–3016.;
www.americanexpress.com

MasterCard
☎ 1-800/MC–ASSIST;
www.mastercard.com

Visa
☎ 1-866/639–1911;
www.visa.com

Road breakdown
☎ 800/CAA-HELP or
514/861–1313

EMERGENCY NUMBERS

Police, fire, ambulance
☎ 911 or dial 0 for the operator who will connect you.

Lost property:
bus or Métro ✉ Mezzanine Level, Berri-UQAM Métro Station ☎ 514/786–4636;
taxis ☎ 514/280–6660
Elsewhere contact the MUC Police ☎ 514/280–4636

US Consulate
✉ 1155 rue Saint-Alexandre
☎ 514/398–9695

US Embassy
✉ 490 Sussex Drive, Ottawa
☎ 613/238–5335;
www.usembassycanada.gov

UK Consulate ✉ 1000 rue de la Gauchetiére
☎ 514/866–5863

British Embassy
✉ 80 Elgin Street, Ottawa
☎ 613/237–1530;
www.britaincanada.org

Irish Embassy
☎ 613/233–6281;
www.foreignaffairs.gov.ie

Language

BASIC VOCABULARY	
oui/ non	yes/no
s'il vous plaît	please
merci	thank you
excusez-moi	excuse me
bonjour	hello
bonsoir	good evening
au revoir	goodbye
parlez-vous anglais?	do you speak English?
je ne comprends pas	I don't understand
combien?	how much?
où est/sont...?	where is/are...?
ici/là	here/there
tournez à gauche/droite	turn left/right
tout droit	straight on
quand?	when?
aujourd'hui	today
hier	yesterday
demain	tomorrow
combien de temps?	how long?
à quelle heure?	at what time?
à quelle heure ouvrez/ fermez-vous?	what time do you open/ close?
avez-vous...?	do you have...?
une chambre simple	a single room
une chambre double	a double room
avec/sans salle de bains	with/without bathroom
le petit déjeuner	breakfast
le déjeuner	lunch
le dîner	dinner
c'est combien?	how much is this?
acceptez-vous des cartes de credit?	do you take credit cards?
j'ai besoin d'un médecin/dentiste	I need a doctor/ dentist
pouvez-vous m'aider?	can you help me?
où est l'hôpital?	where is the hospital?
où est le commissariat?	where is the police station?

NUMBERS	
un	1
deux	2
trois	3
quatre	4
cinq	5
six	6
sept	7
huit	8
neuf	9
dix	10
onze	11
douze	12
treize	13
quatorze	14
quinze	15
seize	16
dix-sept	17
dix-huit	18
dix-neuf	19
vingt	20
vingt-et-un	21
trente	30
quarante	40
cinquante	50
soixante	60
soixante-dix	70
quatre-vingts	80
quatre-vingt- dix	90
cent	100
mille	1,000

Timeline

EARLY DAYS

In 1535 French explorer Jacques Cartier became the first European to set foot in the native village of Hochelaga, the site of modern-day Montréal. He named the hill above the village Mont-Royal—this was translated to Mont-Real by Italian writer G. B. Ramuso in 1556.

FUR CONFLICTS

Montréal was the staging ground of the only Confederate raid on New England during the Civil War in the United States. On October 19, 1864, 20 cavalrymen swooped down on St. Albans, Vermont. The raiders robbed three banks and made off with more than $200,000 before the stunned Vermonters could react. The raiders were arrested in Montréal.

1642 Paul de Chomedey, a French soldier, establishes Ville-Marie on the island of Montréal. He is helped by Jeanne Mance.

1663 King Louis XIV gives land rights on Île de Mont-Real to the Sulpicians, a religious order trying to convert the native population, aided by vision-seeing Marguerite de Bourgeoys.

1682 Ville-Marie becomes HQ of the Compagnie du Nord, fur-trading rivals of the Hudson's Bay Company.

1701 The French sign a treaty with the native Iroquois, ending over 50 years of conflict following the Iroquois massacre of the Hurons, allies of the French, in 1649.

1710 The name Ville-Marie is dropped.

1754–63 The French and Indian War breaks out between England and France. In 1759 General James Wolfe is mortally wounded during the capture of French Québec and in 1760 the British take Montréal. The 1763 Treaty of Paris ends the war and cedes Canada to Britain.

1775 American revolutionary troops occupy Montréal in an effort to enlist French Canadians to their cause.

1832 Montréal is North America's second largest city.

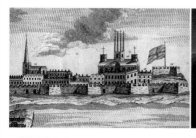

1844 Montréal becomes the capital of the new United Province of Canada.

1867 The Dominion of Canada is formed: Québec, Ontario, New Brunswick, Nova Scotia.

1874 Parc Mont Royal is laid out by Frederick Law Olmsted.

1940 Colorful mayor Camillien Houde is interned after urging Canadians not to register for wartime conscription.

1959 The St. Lawrence Seaway opens.

1969 Canada's federal government accepts both French and English as official languages.

1970 Nationalist terrorists kidnap a provincial cabinet minister and a British diplomat, triggering one of Canada's worst political crises. Québec government makes French the province's only official language.

1995 50 per cent of Québécois vote to remain part of Canada, but in Montréal almost 70 percent vote against independence for the province.

2002 All 24 municipalities on the Island of Montréal merge into one super city.

2005 Allegations of federal corruption over funds destined for Québec reignite the separation issue.

ACHIEVEMENTS

● The opening of the Lachine Canal in 1825 allows ships to travel between the Atlantic and the Great Lakes.

● The completion of the Canadian Pacific Railway in 1886 links Montréal to the Pacific coast, helping the city to develop into the financial and industrial capital of Canada.

● Montréal's Expo '67 world fair, celebrating Canada's centennial, attracts 53 million visitors.

● Montréal hosts the summer Olympic Games in 1976.

A view of early Montréal and fortifications (far left)
A portrait of Major General, James Wolfe (middle left)
A picture depicts the death of General Wolfe (middle right)
Montréal in winter, an ice jam (right)

Index

CITYPACK TOP 25
Montréal

WRITTEN BY Tim Jepson
DESIGN CONCEPT AND DESIGN WORK Kate Harling
INDEXER Marie Lorimer
EDITORIAL MANAGEMENT Apostrophe S Limited
SERIES EDITOR Paul Mitchell

© **AUTOMOBILE ASSOCIATION DEVELOPMENTS LIMITED 2007**
First published 1997
Colour separation by Keenes
Printed and bound by Leo, China

A CIP catalogue record for this book is available from the British Library.

ISBN 978-0-7495-5090-5

Published by AA Publishing, a trading name of Automobile Association Developments Limited, whose registered office is Fanum House, Basing View, Basingstoke, Hampshire RG21 4EA. Registered number 1878835.

A02815
Maps in this title produced from mapping © MAIRDUMONT / Falk Verlag 2006
Transport map © Communicarta Ltd, UK

The Automobile Association would like to thank the following photographers, companies and picture libraries for their assistance in the preparation of this book.

Abbreviations for the picture credits are as follows – (t) top; (b) bottom; (c) centre; (l) left; (r) right; (AA) AA World Travel Library.

Front cover image: Canadian Tourism Commission, Pierre St-Jacques
Back cover images : (t) AA/J F Pin, (tc) AA/C Sawyer, (bc) AA/R Elliot, (b) AA/J F Pin

Inside F/C(1) Montréal Botanical Garden; **(2)** AA/J F Pin; **(3)** Tourisme Montréal, Stéphan Poulin; **(4)** McCord Museum of Canadian History; **(5)** AA/J F Pin; **(6)** AA/J F Pin; **(7)** Régie des installations Olympiques; **(8)** Tourisme Montréal, Stéphan Poulin; **(9)** Grand Prix F1 of Canada; **(10)** AA/J F Pin. **1** Tourisme Montréal, Stéphan Poulin; **2/3t** Tourisme Montréal; **4/5t** Tourisme Montréal; **4tl** AA/C Coe; **5b** AA/J F Pin; **6/7t** Tourisme Montréal; **6cl** Pierre Girard; **6c** AA/J F Pin; **6cr** AA/J F Pin; **6bl** AA/J F Pin; **6bc** AA/J F Pin; **6br** Canadian Tourism Commission, Pierre St-Jacques; **7cl** Tourisme Montréal; **7c** AA/J F Pin; **7cr** AA/N Sumner; **7bl** Biodôme de Montréal; **7bc** AA/J F Pin; **7br** Les Ballets Jazz de Montréal, Nicole Rivelli; **8/9t** Tourisme Montréal; **10/1t** Tourisme Montréal; **10tr** Tourisme Montréal, Stéphan Poulin; **10cr** Tourisme Montréal, Stéphan Poulin; **10bcr** Mark Tomalty; **10br** AA/M Dent; **11tl** Tourisme Montréal, Stéphan Poulin; **11cl** Tourisme Québec, Linda Turgeon; **11bl** AA/C Coe; **12/3t** Tourisme Montréal; **12b** Tourisme Montréal, Stéphan Poulin; **13tl** Tourisme Montréal, Stéphan Poulin; **13tcl** Casino de Montréal; **13cl** AA/J F Pin; **13bcl** Les Ballets Jazz de Montréal, Nicole Rivelli; **13b** Canadian Tourism Commission, Pierre St-Jacques; **14/5t** Tourisme Montréal; **14tr** AA/P Kenward; **14cr** Tourisme Montréal, Stéphan Poulin; **14bcr** Tourisme Montréal, Stéphan Poulin; **14br** Tourisme Montréal, Stéphan Poulin; **15br** Nuances Restaurant, Casino de Montréal; **16/7t** Tourisme Montréal; **16tr** Tourisme Montréal, Stéphan Poulin; **16cr** AA/J F Pin; **16br** Canadian Tourism Commission, Pierre St-Jacques; **17tl** Tourisme Montréal, Stéphan Poulin; **17tcl** Nuances Restaurant, Casino de Montréal; **17bcl** Hotel St-Paul; **17bl** Tourisme Montréal, Stéphan Poulin; **18t** Tourisme Montréal; **18tr** Tourisme Montréal, Stéphan Poulin; **18tcr** Photodisc; **18bcr** Tourisme Montréal, Stéphan Poulin; **18br** AA/J F Pin; **19t** Tourisme Montréal, Stéphan Poulin; **19tc** AA/J F Pin; **19c** Tourisme Montréal; **19bc** AA/J F Pin; **19b** Parc Jean-Drapeau, Bernard Brault; **20/1** Tourisme Montréal, Stéphan Poulin; **24t** Canadian Tourism Commission, Pierre St-Jacques; **24/5t** AA/J F Pin; **26tl** Tourisme Montréal, Stéphan Poulin; **26tr** AA/J F Pin; **27tl** AA/J F Pin; **27tr** Centre d'histoire de Montréal; **28tl** AA/J F Pin; **28tc** AA/J F Pin; **28tr** AA/J F Pin; **29tl** Parks Canada; **29tr** AA/J F Pin; **30/1t** www.old.montréal.qc.ca, le photographe masqué; **31t** A.P.E.S., Anton Fercher; **32l** Pointe-à-Callière, Montréal Museum of Archaeology and History, Roderick Chen; **32/3c** AA/J F Pin; **33r** Tourisme Montréal, Stéphan Poulin; **34tl** AA/J F Pin; **34tr** Pierre Girard; **35t** AA/J F Pin; **35b** Tourisme Montréal, Stéphan Poulin; **36bl** AA/J F Pin; **36/7t** AA/J F Pin; **37bl** AA/J F Pin; **37b** Tourisme Montréal, Stéphan Poulin; **38t** AA/J F Pin; **38b** AA/J F Pin; **39t** AA/J F Pin; **40t** Tourisme Montréal, Stéphan Poulin; **41t** AA/M Chaplow; **42t** Tourisme Montréal, Stéphan Poulin; **43t** AA/C Sawyer; **44t** Tourisme Montréal, Stéphan Poulin; **45** AA/J F Pin; **48** AA/J F Pin; **49tl** AA/J F Pin; **49tr** AA/J F Pin; **50tl** AA/J F Pin; **50tr** Canadian Tourism Commission, Pierre St-Jacques; **51tl** AA/J F Pin; **51tr** Cöpilia; **52** AA/J F Pin; **52/3t** McCord Museum of Canadian History; **52/3b** AA/J F Pin; **53** AA/J F Pin; **54** Hisham Ibrahim/Photov.com/Alamy; **54/5** Sean O'Neill; **56/7** Tourisme Montréal, Daniel Choinière; **57** Tourisme Montréal, Stéphan Poulin; **58/9t** AA/J F Pin; **58b** www.old.montréal.qc.ca, le photographe masqué; **59bl** Tourisme Montréal, Stéphan Poulin; **59br** Montréal Planétarium; **60** AA/J F Pin; **61** Tourisme Montréal, Stéphan Poulin; **62t** Tourisme Montréal, Stéphan Poulin; **63t** Photodisc; **64t** AA/J F Pin; **65t** Photodisc; **66t** Tourisme Québec, Linda Turgeon; **67** Tourisme Montréal, Stéphan Poulin; **70/1** McGill University's Residence Halls; **71** Tourisme Montréal, Stéphan Poulin; **72** Tourisme Montréal; **72/3t** Tourisme Montréal, Stéphan Poulin; **72/3bl** Tourisme Montréal, Stéphan Poulin; **73br** AA/J F Pin; **74l** AA/J F Pin; **74r** AA/J F Pin; **75t** AA/J F Pin; **75b** Marie-Claude Guyon et Audrey Rainville; **76t** AA/J F Pin; **76b** Tourisme Montréal, Stéphan Poulin; **77t** AA/J F Pin; **78t** Tourisme Montréal, Stéphan Poulin; **79t** Photodisc; **80t** Digitalvision; **81t** Tourisme Québec, Linda Turgeon; **82t** AA/C Sawyer; **83** Montréal Biodôme, Sean O' Neill; **86** Régie des installations Olympiques; **87l** Régie des installations Olympiques; **87r** AA/J F Pin; **88tl** AA/J F Pin; **88bl** Biodôme de Montréal; **88/9tc** Canadian Tourism Commission, Pierre St-Jacques; **88/9bc** AA/J F Pin; **89bl** Montréal Biodôme, Sean O' Neill; **89r** AA/J F Pin; **90lt** Montréal Botanical Garden, Michel Tremblay; **90bl** Montréal Botanical Garden, Michel Tremblay; **90br** Montréal Botanical Garden; **91t** AA/J F Pin; **91bl** Montréal Botanical Garden, Michel Tremblay; **91br** AA/N Sumner; **92t** AA/J F Pin; **92b** Gilles Rivest; **93** Montréal Botanical Garden; **94t** AA/J F Pin; **94b** Tourisme Montréal, Stéphan Poulin; **95** AA/J F Pin; **98tl** Canadian Centre for Architecture, Richard Bryant; **98/9tc** Canadian Centre for Architecture, Richard Paré, 1989; **99tr** Canadian Centre for Architecture, Richard Bryant; **100tl** Grand Prix F1 of Canada; **100tr** AA/J F Pin; **101tl** Tourisme Montréal, Stéphan Poulin; **101tr** AA/J F Pin; **102tl** AA/J F Pin; **102/3t** Canadian Tourism Commission, Pierre St-Jacques; **104t** Le Bateau-Mouche au Vieux-Port de Montréal, Yves Binette; **105** AA/J F Pin; **106t** AA/J F Pin; **106b** Dan Lavoie (Studio Odyssée); **107** AA/J F Pin; **108/9t** AA/C Sawyer; **108tcl** Inter-Continental Montréal; **108c** Hotel St-Paul; **108bcr** Hotel St-Paul; **108br** Tourisme Montréal, Stéphan Poulin; **110/1t** AA/C Sawyer; **112t** AA/C Sawyer; **113** Tourisme Montréal, Stéphan Poulin; **114/5t** AA/J F Pin; **116/7t** AA/J F Pin; **117cl** AA/R Elliot; **117bl** AA/R Elliot; **118/9t** AA/J F Pin; **120/1t** AA/J F Pin; **122t** AA/J F Pin; **123** Tourisme Montréal, Stéphan Poulin; **124/5t** AA/J F Pin; **124bl** AA; **124br** AA; **124/5bc** AA; **125br** AA.

Every effort has been made to trace the copyright holders, and we apologise in advance for any accidental errors. We would be happy to apply the corrections in the following edition of this publication.